HOW TO BE CREATIVE IN TEXTILE ART

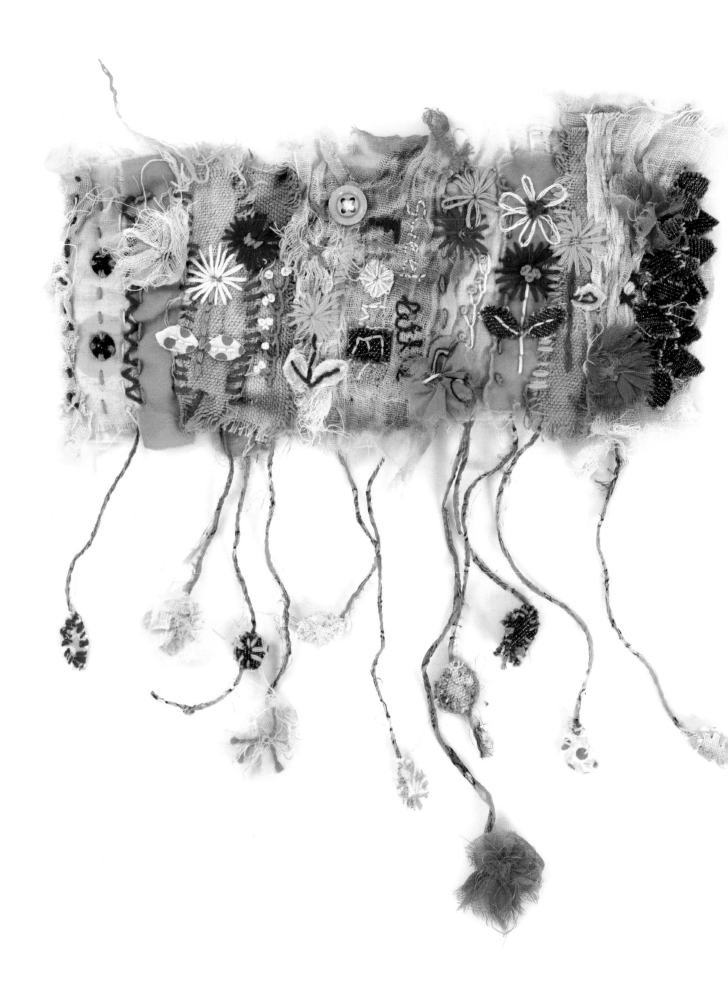

HOW TO BE CREATIVE IN TEXTILE ART

JULIA TRISTON   RACHEL LOMBARD

BATSFORD

For Nick and Zoë and Tim – without your love, support, constant encouragement and understanding, this book would not have been possible. Thanks for being there. To the memory of Maud and Tim Tratt – inspirational, creative grandparents who always encouraged me to believe in myself.
Julia Triston

For all my family, near and far, you are a continuous source of joy and inspiration! To the memory of my beloved Dad, Sidney John Sutherland – this book would have made him proud.
Rachel Lombard

First published in the United Kingdom in 2011 by
Batsford, 10 Southcombe Street, London W14 0RA

An imprint of Anova Books Company Ltd

Copyright © Batsford 2011
Text copyright © Julia Triston and Rachel Lombard 2011

ISBN 9781849940061

A CIP catalogue record for this book is available from the British Library.
18 17 16 15 14 13 12 11
10 9 8 7 6 5 4 3 2 1

Reproduction by Dot Gradations Ltd, UK
Printed and bound by Craft Print International Ltd, Singapore

Page 1: **Experimental Edges** (Ali Kent, Caroline Pinnington, Janice MacDougall, Julia Triston, Rachel Lombard) Hand and machine embroidery on various fabrics and papers to create edges for textile projects. Page 2: **Decorative Cuff** (Karine Richardson). Hand embroidery on hand-dyed fabrics. Page 3, top: **Three Covered Buttons** (Rachel Lombard). Machine and hand stitch on silk. Bottom: **Tutti Frutti Brooch** (Julia Triston). Hand stitch and buttons on a constructed background. Left: **Wrought sample** (Rachel Lombard) (see page 79).
Right: **Shoes** (Pauline Twyman). Free machine embroidery and embellishments on base of moulded cotton wool paper.

CONTENTS

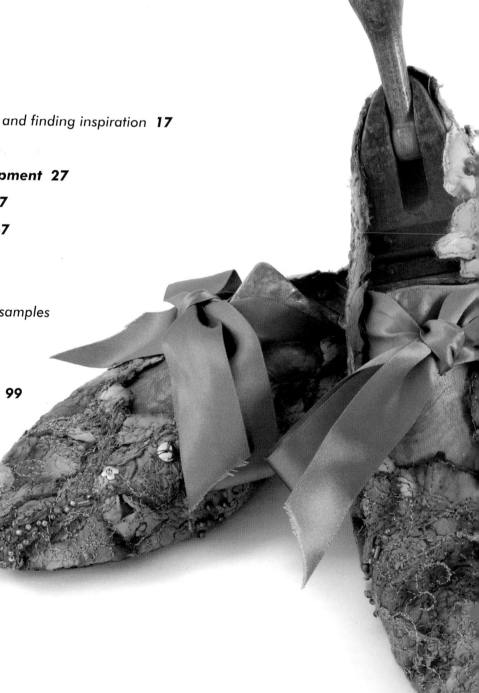

FOREWORD

We believe that everyone has the ability to develop work that expresses their individual creativity, although many people lack the confidence to interpret their ideas. By challenging existing ways of working and offering refreshing and accessible alternatives, *How to be Creative in Textile Art* will give you the tools to develop and enjoy the creativity that is innate in everyone.

While we can all be told how to do or make something, there is an exciting world beyond, based on your own ideas, your own sources, and your own references and preferences – things that are important and significant to you.

Beginning with your personal starting points, this book will guide and support you through the processes of creating a successful and rewarding piece of work – from selecting viable ideas and design development to completion and evaluation – enabling you to find your own creative solutions in the process of stitch and design.

Whether your projects are big or small, two- or three-dimensional, traditional or contemporary, *How to be Creative in Textile Art* will encourage you to ask questions and to examine different methods of exploring ideas for stitching, so that you can challenge yourself, develop your own individual style, discover innovative solutions, and pursue your chosen themes with confidence. Enjoy your unique creative journey and celebrate its expression through your own stitched textiles.

How many times have you been to an exhibition and said to yourself, 'I wish I could do that!' or 'I wish I'd thought of that!'? This is a very common occurrence, and the first thing to bear in mind is that however experienced the artist may be, everyone has to start at the beginning for each new body of work. The second thing to consider is that art is a reflection of the person creating it and your artwork will be a reflection of you. Engaging with your creativity and making a start is the difficult bit, but as you have picked up this book, you are already committed to taking the first steps.

Many people approach their textile project with a finished item in mind. This is an 'end-loaded' approach. This book will encourage you to make a start on your textile project (from your chosen theme) and develop your ideas as you work until a resolution for your final piece evolves. This is a 'front-loaded' approach and we will demonstrate how, by following the procedures in this book, this will enable you to develop a more expressive and richer body of work.

How to be Creative in Textile Art sets out a framework to guide you step by step through the processes of exploring, developing, making and evaluating your own stitched-textile project, placing an emphasis on the creative personal journey itself, rather than focusing on the finished project. We live in a busy world and finding time to be creative can be a struggle. By breaking down a project into a series of manageable stages, the whole process will become more achievable and less daunting.

Your creative journey is not just about the physical making of your textile project. Spending time looking at and thinking about your work is a necessary part of the process too, and should never be underestimated – this reflective practice will enable you to harness your creativity constructively. So remember, next time you go to an exhibition: be inspired not intimidated – you can do it too!

Left: **Clutch bag** (Karine Richardson). Free machine embroidery, hand stitch and embellishments on pieced and dissolvable fabrics. Above: **Handmade tassel** (Janice MacDougall). Silk sari waste and wooden beads.

PART 1 : GATHERING

Chapter 1

WHERE TO START?

turning your ideas into a project

selecting a theme and setting your boundaries

the purpose of a sketchbook

Left: **Lace Book** (Julia Triston).
Exploration of lace patterns:
detail of overlapping cut,
shaped, printed and stitched
sketchbook pages.

This chapter is about taking your first steps towards being creative with textiles and stitch. It will lead you through the early stages of how to choose a personal theme for your work and how to start the process of working directly and confidently into a sketchbook. This will enable you to generate ideas that will feed into, and enrich, your textile work.

Turning your ideas into a project

Ideas need to be turned into reality, and to realize your textile project it is important to choose a theme or source that appeals to you and captures your imagination. This will make the creative process easier and more enjoyable.

Keeping a sketchbook will enable you to have a personal creative space where everything relevant to your project can be stored. In your sketchbook you can:

- gather information
- record
- evaluate
- order
- reference
- sketch
- stitch
- list and keep notes

Right: **Beauty Sketchbook** (Rachel Lombard). Explores how cosmetics are packaged and how the idea of beauty is presented. Opposite page: **Colour Sketchbook** (Julia Triston). Pages show design development work of overlaying colour on colour.

one step further . . . . .

textured hand-made paper Deka stripes +
stabilotone pencil spots + lines over surface

textured
hand made paper with leaves – painted
with Deka silk paint stripes (+ pencil
(stabilotone) motifs over top when dried)

textured handmade fibre paper, as above
+ opposite but also with maikal, too.

Selecting a theme and setting your boundaries

Having a theme running through your sketchbook is essential to the development of an interesting and individual body of work. Setting yourself some boundaries will enable you to focus on what to include and what to leave out. Surprisingly, you can be more creative if you impose limitations on yourself and narrow your options down. The table below shows how you can select a broad theme, break it down to a more specific focus, then further refine it into smaller, more manageable elements.

THEME	FOCUS	ELEMENTS
architecture	Durham Cathedral	pillars archways weathered stone doorways door knockers stained-glass windows ecclesiastical vestments
	cityscapes	grids in high-rise blocks drain covers railings shop signs decorative tiles people reflections
nature	seaside	tidal marks and ripples ice cream and candy floss rockpools seaweed sand dunes flotsam and jetsam
	birds	feathers flight patterns nests eggs tracks
clothing	uniforms	braiding buttons pocket details headwear fastenings surface details badges

The purpose of a sketchbook

Starting a sketchbook is both scary and exciting. Being faced with blank sheet after blank sheet can be a daunting prospect for some people, but can offer an inviting freedom for others. Sketchbooks are a personal space, and can be an entirely private one, somewhere to consider possibilities, develop and investigate your options, and resolve your ideas through exploration and experimentation. You do not have to show your sketchbook to anyone else.

Choosing a sketchbook

There is a vast range of sketchbooks to choose from, so how do you know which one will be right for you? Here are some points to consider:

Below: **Atlas Sketchbook** (Rachel Lombard). Made from a third of an old atlas's cover and torn pages. Hand and machine stitch with mother-of-pearl buttons.

- the shape or format of the sketchbook – square, rectangular, portrait, landscape or defined (for example, leaf-shaped, heart-shaped). What is appealing to you? What is appropriate for your content?
- the size of the sketchbook. Remember that it is easier to transport smaller sketchbooks, but smaller pages can limit the size of your drawings or your insertions within the pages.
- the binding – a ring-bound sketchbook offers the possibility of easier page turning, but a ready-glued, perfect-bound pad is often much cheaper.
- the pages – thick pages or thin ones? Handmade and irregular paper, or smooth and consistent surfaces? White, cream, buff, black or coloured pages?
- cost – you do not have to buy a purpose-made sketchbook at all. You could make your own from lining paper, or from an old atlas, wallpaper sample books or recycled textbook pages.

Tips on keeping a sketchbook

Once you've chosen your sketchbook you might find the following tips handy, to help you to use it effectively:

- always start a few pages in – this gives you the opportunity to fill in the first few pages with titles or content listings when you have finished your project. If you don't use them, you can always tear them out.
- you don't have to work pages consecutively.
- don't be too precious with your pages – if you make a mistake, leave it in and come back to it later; it may be that you can work something over the top of it or layer it with another drawing or sample.
- try rotating your sketchbook to work from different angles and directions.
- remember that some pages will always be more successful than others.
- you can start two different ideas from opposite ends of your sketchbook.
- don't go back and take things out – each page is a record of where you were then, not where you are now.

Being creative with your sketchbook

Many sketchbook users choose to work straight on to white pages. Others prefer to colour, shape or decorate their pages before working into them. Pages can be enhanced by:

- folding to form flaps and hidden spaces.
- cutting or tearing vertically or horizontally.
- cutting or tearing away to add interest.
- gluing, taping and stitching additions to extend the original page.
- gluing or stitching together to make pockets for templates and patterns.
- colouring with inks, tea bags, diluted paints, etc.
- cutting out windows to reveal layers beneath.
- stiffening – try emulsion, varnish or acrylic paint.
- altering the edges – try shaping with scissors or tearing more randomly.

Essentially, sketchbooks are places to record and to experiment with your ideas. There is no right or wrong way to keep them. Beginning a sketchbook is the same as beginning an adventure – you know your starting point, but you never know quite where it is going to take you.

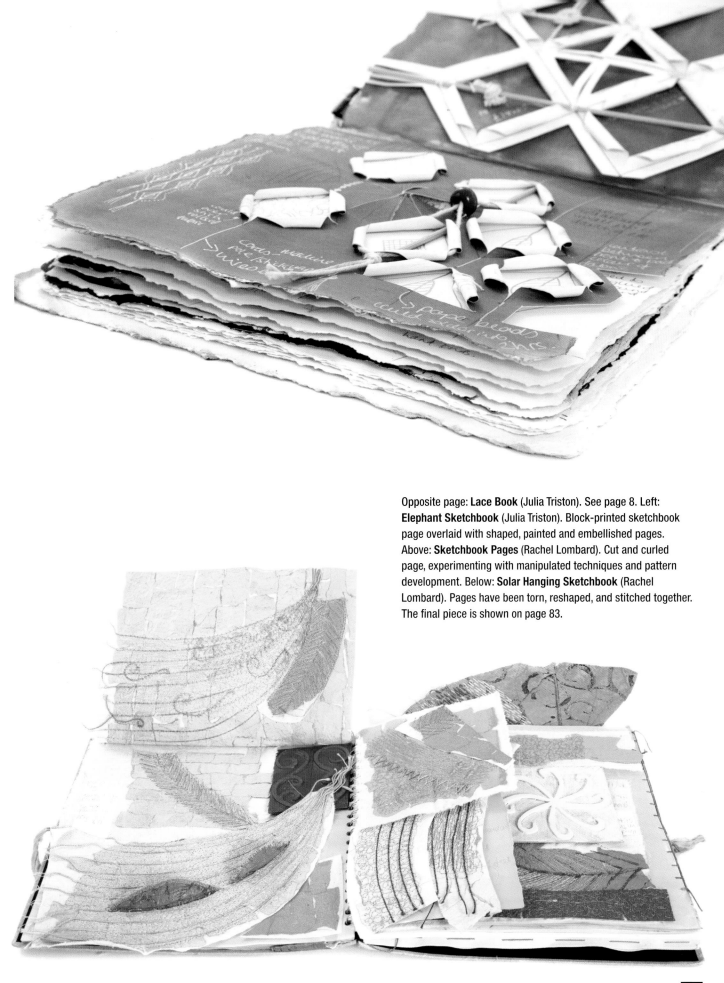

Opposite page: **Lace Book** (Julia Triston). See page 8. Left: **Elephant Sketchbook** (Julia Triston). Block-printed sketchbook page overlaid with shaped, painted and embellished pages. Above: **Sketchbook Pages** (Rachel Lombard). Cut and curled page, experimenting with manipulated techniques and pattern development. Below: **Solar Hanging Sketchbook** (Rachel Lombard). Pages have been torn, reshaped, and stitched together. The final piece is shown on page 83.

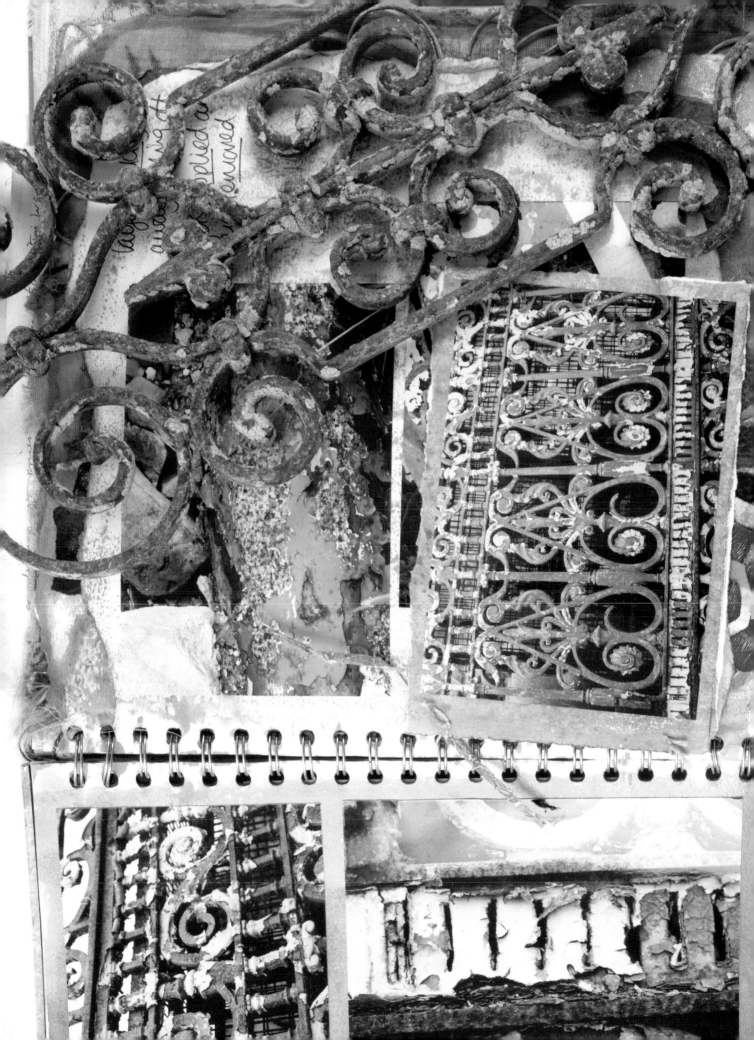

Chapter 2

SEARCHING FOR A SOURCE AND FINDING INSPIRATION

using titles as a starting point

gathering source material

your personal environment

out and about

conclusion to Part 1

Left: **Wrought Sketchbook** (Rachel Lombard). Primary source materials, wrought iron panel, photographs.

In Chapter 1 we looked at ways to begin a sketchbook. This chapter is about exploring your ideas, making choices and clarifying your starting points. Starting a project can feel daunting, but if you break it down into smaller and logical parts, it becomes more manageable and a less overwhelming task.

Using titles as a starting point

Having a 'working title' for your textile project enables you to focus your thoughts on collecting relevant materials, information and ideas. Your working title may not be the one you end up with, as titles can shift and change as you review and refine your work, but it will give you a starting point, which will enable you to clarify your thoughts and processes from the outset.

A title is sometimes given to you for a competition, exhibition or commission, or it may be something you set yourself as a personal or group challenge. Your own title can emerge after you have seen an inspiring exhibition or another artist's body of work.

Start to think of what interests you and why. It is important that the title you choose inspires you – if you have no passion for your title, this will show in your final work.

Here are some possibilities for titles:

- Organic Formations
- The Seven Deadly Sins
- Feasts and Festivals
- Folds and Creases
- Urban Landscapes
- Edges and Adornment
- Inside Out
- Time and Tide
- Revealed and Concealed

Words can also be used as starting points. Here are a few suggestions:

- structures
- identity
- generation
- montage
- transformation
- memories
- layers
- crossroads
- decay

Choosing a title is the beginning of defining a personal interpretation of a theme, which will set the boundaries for the next stages of development in design and sampling.

Mind maps

A good way to start organizing your thoughts is to create a mind map. This is a means of recording your ideas in one place, giving an overview of all the possibilities and avenues to investigate that stem from a central theme or title. It is a visual way of thinking, and represents your ideas and the personal links and connections that need to make sense only to you. A mind map will help you to expand your ways of thinking, generate further ideas, and begin to shape and structure the way you approach your project. It is an opportunity to see all of the threads of your ideas together and to work out where the links lie. A mind map can include and make reference to:

- associated words, phrases and translations
- images, drawings and doodles
- synonyms and antonyms
- synaesthesia
- the senses – sight, hearing, taste, smell, touch and kinaesthesia
- book titles
- song lyrics
- memories
- dreams
- people and personalities
- the design elements – colour, line, shape, form and texture
- places
- seasons
- emotions and feelings
- moods
- climate
- raw materials
- found objects

Your mind map will be a useful tool, becoming part of your source material and a point of reference at different stages of your project. Noting down your thoughts in this way gives you the freedom to explore all your ideas, however tenuous, broadening your outlook and possibly pushing you in unexpected directions. There are no boundaries when creating your mind map, and committing your ideas to paper will enable you to see physically the links and connections between your different strands of thought. Not all of your ideas will ultimately be useful, but others will become more significant.

Your mind map does not have to be neat and tidy, nor does it have to be in a particular order. It can take different forms. Once created, however, it is important to keep it accessible for easy reference – we suggest pinning it up on a notice board or a wall that you regularly see. That way you will keep your ideas present in your mind, and continually reflect on your progress.

Don't be afraid to add or take away points, or move them about – your mind map is an expression of *your* ideas, which you will interpret from *your* thoughts.

Gathering source material

You should gather as much inspiring source material as possible. Having a mixture of primary and secondary sources is essential, as this is a further important stage of exploring and thinking; it will encourage you to develop your theme laterally as well as literally, opening up new realms of creativity. Good research will give you a store of information to call upon and refer to as you move through your creative process.

Primary sources

Primary research is a collection of information generated or initiated yourself – it is a direct and personal response to your theme and source material. It could be a sketch, a drawing, a photograph or some notes gathered from an interview. When using primary sources you are processing information just for yourself; it is gathered from your individual point of view. No one else will look at an object, observe it and record it like you do. Take time to give yourself space to really look at, think about and experience your source.

Secondary sources

Above: Secondary Sources (Julia Triston). Magazines, postcards, catalogues, leaflets, paint charts etc. Below: **Time and Tide** (Rachel Lombard). Primary sources, sketches and experimental stitched samples.

Secondary research is a collection of information gathered from sources that already exist. These could be postcards of other artists' work, magazines, books, the Internet or exhibition catalogues. When using secondary source material some of the processing has already been done for you; it is someone else's recorded image, point of view, work or idea. Secondary research allows you to see how others have interpreted the same, or a similar, theme.

The table shown on the opposite page gives many examples of the distinctions between primary and secondary source materials. Working from the central theme of your mind map, begin to explore and gather as much source material as possible. By looking at the familiar in a more enquiring way, you will discover that inspiration is all around you and endless opportunities for creative exploration will present themselves.

TITLE	INSPIRATION	PRIMARY SOURCE	SECONDARY SOURCE
Revealed and Concealed	an exhibition of masks	drawing the masks in your sketchbook annotating the mask details in your sketchbook, and your response to them interviewing the mask makers and exhibition curator photographing the exhibits comparing notes with other exhibition visitors	buying the exhibition catalogue and postcards of the masks reading reviews of the exhibition researching further historical sources for more information on the masks from books or via the Internet
Time and Tide	a visit to the seaside	collecting raw materials – shells, pebbles, driftwood, etc. photographing sand patterns taking rubbings from the rock surfaces drawing and sculpting in the sand writing a poem on the beach, recording your feelings gathering mementoes of the experience – lollipop sticks, boat tickets, old swimming costumes	collating old family photographs of seaside holidays collaging holiday brochures, posters and postcards reading poems about the seaside
Identity	the kitchen workspace	photographing food colouring your sketchbook pages with spices staining your fabric with tea or coffee stitching together a patchwork of vegetable skins to create a surface weaving into vegetable or fruit netting printing with kitchen utensils recycling packaging to use as embellishments – for example, bottle tops and labels	reading recipe books watching TV chef programmes researching food politics collating information from wartime ration books in family archives collecting family recipes reading memoirs of chefs, cooks and housekeepers researching language references – for example, 'upper crust', 'salt of the earth'

Your personal environment

It is easy to overlook your personal environment as a source of inspiration for your textile art projects. Great artworks have been created from ordinary everyday objects. Such items can provide rich source material for creative people in all disciplines.

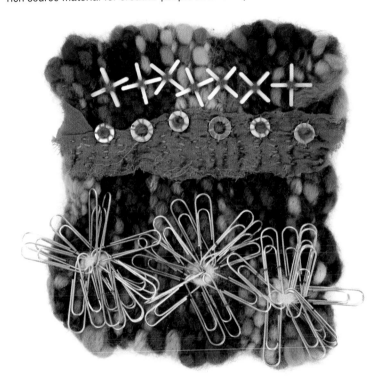

Above left: **Darning (detail)** (Mandy Pattullo). Hand stitch and haberdashery items on reclaimed embroidery. Left: **Sample panel (detail)** (Cas Holmes) Layered paper bags and magazine pages with hand and machine stitch. Above: **Summer Garden** (Julieanne Long). Knitted background with everyday objects attached with hand stitch. Right: **Heather Landscape** (Liz Reed). Reclaimed sweaters, felted and manipulated with hand stitch.

We all store and order the things around us – for example, our plans and appointments on a family calendar or thoughts and ideas in a personal diary. Whether consciously or not, we all create collections within our personal environments, such as seed packets in the garden shed, cutlery and spices in the kitchen drawer, linen in the airing cupboard, pots of paint in the garage or trinkets in the jewellery box.

What do your collections say about you?

Looking closely at what you have gathered around you can reveal a continuity that you may have previously been unaware of. For example:

- do you favour one colour palette over another?
- do you like a minimalist environment or one that is highly decorative?
- does a theme emerge from your collections?
- what initially inspired you to buy, keep and collect these particular items?
- are your collections deliberate (for example, specialist tools in a box) or accidental (for example, a collection of bus tickets and receipts at the bottom of your handbag)?

Taking the time really to look and see what is around you can open your mind to a new world of possibilities and sources of inspiration.

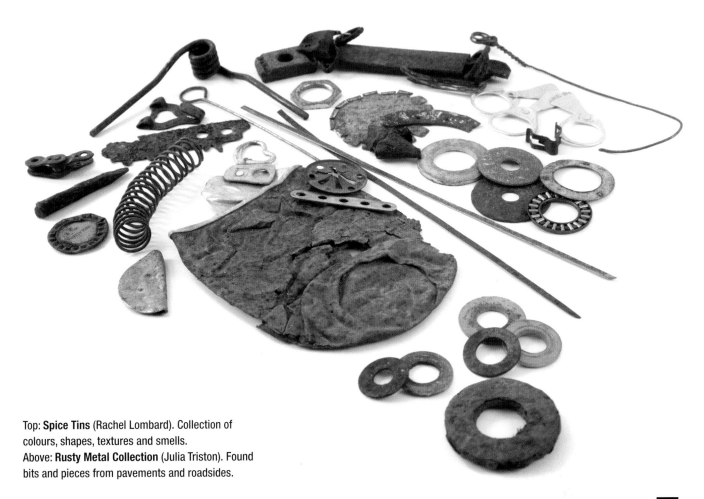

Top: **Spice Tins** (Rachel Lombard). Collection of colours, shapes, textures and smells.
Above: **Rusty Metal Collection** (Julia Triston). Found bits and pieces from pavements and roadsides.

Out and about

There is a wealth of source material to discover in the wider world. We are all so busy hurrying from one place to another that we are not always aware of what is going on or changing around us. We all have outside spaces that become so familiar that we cease to really see them. Consider the distinctions between the different types of environments around you – some are far more managed and built up, while others are wilder and more natural.

Above: **Norway Sketchbook** (Rachel Lombard). Textured samples developed from photograph of bark detail. Opposite page: **Toran Sketchbook** (Julia Triston). Analysing possible colourways and surface details for Toran, shown on page 114–115.

Looking at the familiar in detail

When you are out and about, get into the habit of observing the details in your immediate surroundings that you usually overlook:

- do you notice patterns around you in drain covers or in tree branches against the sky?
- how many different shades of red can you see in the brickwork around you?
- do you notice gradual seasonal changes in the leaves, in the light, and in the way people dress?
- are you aware of what is permanent and what is transitory around you?
- can you spot ten new details on your journey to work, or when out for a walk?

Learning to look attentively is a vital skill in developing your creativity. There are many ways to extend your observational skills. For example, get into the habit of:

- carrying a sketchbook to record, draw, sketch and annotate what's around you.
- photographing your surroundings from different angles – for example, sitting on the floor to capture your image.
- focusing on the detail, not just the periphery, of an area or subject.
- breaking things down into components – a tree, for instance, is composed of bark, leaves, seeds, flowers, fruits, lichen, moss, fungus, parasites, and each has its own quality.
- looking up to notice what you have not seen before – for example, details of stonework, windows and gargoyles.
- looking down to examine what is usually taken for granted – for example, the pattern of footprints or the detail in oily or icy puddles.
- analysing the range of colours in your subject – water, for instance, is clear but can appear to be blue, brown, green, black or white.
- looking for new things every day.
- being aware of the silhouettes formed by objects.
- noticing the shadows, gaps and negative spaces that exist around objects.
- visiting the same place at a different time of day or year to observe the changes in light, weather and season.

Conclusion to Part 1

Gathering is all about making choices, working out what interests you and collecting together everything you think may be relevant to your textile project. This is your opportunity to explore the depth and breadth of your title or theme. If you think something is appropriate source material at this stage, then include it. Taking time to refer to your mind map will remind you of your original thoughts – you will be amazed at how far your ideas have progressed.

In Part 2 we will show and discuss different ways to explore and develop your source materials and research.

PART 2 : EXPLORATION AND DEVELOPMENT

Chapter 3

MAKING CONNECTIONS

pulling together your collection

mood boards

commonality of themes

investigating the formal elements of design

a framework for composition

Left: **Time and Tide Mood Board**
(Rachel Lombard). Photographs,
flotsam and jetsam from
Northumberland beach walks.

This chapter will encourage you to begin visually exploring your chosen source material and to investigate the formal elements of design, which are the fundamental components in a successful piece of artwork.

Pulling together your collection

Gathering together your source materials can take time and you may have amassed a large and diverse collection of items, including your mind maps, drawings, papers, objects, photographs and notes. Just as jigsaws are made up of a large number of individual pieces that make a complete picture only when they are joined together, your collection of source material will make sense only when you look at it in its entirety and begin working out what goes where and how it fits together.

Starting with everything spread out around you will enable you to have an overview of your gathered materials. Lay everything out, and as you do so, think about what motivated you to choose each piece. This is your opportunity to start working directly with what interests you and to begin to make connections between your sources.

Mood boards

At this point you might find it useful to create a mood board. Mood boards (or inspiration or concept boards) feature displays of gathered information and materials, from both primary and secondary sources, that tell the story of your research. They can conjure up a mood, express a feeling or convey a concept. They can communicate and draw together elements of your chosen theme, colour palette, key words and initial responses to your source material. Your mood board may contain photographs, postcards, magazine cuttings, text, stitch, sketches, tracings and actual source materials (for example, leaves, shells or lace).

Right: **Time and Tide Mood Board** (Rachel Lombard). Opposite page: **Toran Mood Board** (Julia Triston). Gathered primary and secondary sources, many from travels in India, collated for inspiration for Toran (shown on page 114–115).

Commonality of themes

With reference to your mind map and mood board, take time to look closely at your collections and source materials. Move them about, group them thematically – are new and unexpected common themes beginning to emerge? Is there a dominant colour, shape or surface among your collection that you had not previously realized? Spending time handling, reordering and sorting through your materials can result in surprising discoveries that may lead your thought processes in a new direction. Never underestimate the importance of time spent thinking, investigating, playing with and visually exploring your source materials.

Right: **Rusty Metal Collection** (Julia Triston). Composition from arranged and reordered elements of primary source material.

Ideas for visual exploration

Here are some suggestions for how to start discovering something extraordinary in the ordinary:

- look at the backs and insides of your objects, and underneath them, to discover their hidden colours, shapes, patterns and textures.
- look at your object in a mirror – reversed images look surprisingly different.
- examine your object through a magnifying glass – what details do you notice?
- look through a viewfinder – by taking away the distraction of the complete and the obvious, you will be able to focus on smaller isolated areas.
- put your object in a glass of water to produce a distorted image.
- feel your objects with your eyes closed – what surface variations and textures become apparent that you were not conscious of before?

Above: **Tide and Time Collection** (Rachel Lombard). Examining and exploring shapes, patterns and possibilities. Below: Examining beach finds using a reflected and an isolated image (Rachel Lombard).

Below: **Tree Sketchbook** (Jennifer Mary Lehm). Drawings, sketches and stitch explorations. Opposite page, top: **Sketchbook for Cuff** (Karine Richardson). Drawings and stitch sketches for cuff shown on page 2. Middle: **Panel Sketchbook** (Val Arif). Design development work from the Naulakha Pavilion (Palace of Mirrors) in Pakistan. Bottom: **Sketchbook** (Tracy A Franklin). Demonstrating repeat motifs and shaded tones, shadows and colours

Documenting your visual explorations

It is important to record your responses to the visual explorations of your source materials in a variety of ways. For example, you can:

- sketch and draw what you see
- photograph your results
- make notes about your observations, discoveries and decisions

Each way of recording has a different quality – a sketch is a personal interpretation, while a photograph captures an instant in time through a lens. Each method is equally valid and will offer a different perspective and potential for development.

By doing this, your eureka moments will be documented, new thoughts and ideas will not be forgotten, and processes can be recorded, so that they can be repeated if necessary.

Investigating the formal elements of design

The formal elements of design are the components, or building blocks, that make up an overall visual composition and a successful piece of design or artwork.

The five main formal elements of design are:

* colour
* line
* shape
* form
* texture

Having an awareness of these formal elements of design will give you a better understanding of how to create a piece of artwork and a better appreciation of what makes it successful.

Colour wheel (Catherine Gowthorpe). Thread wrappings to show primary, secondary and tertiary colours.

Colour

Colour is the most complex and expressive of the formal elements of design. It has enormous impact and cultural significance. Colour can be used to heighten visual contrasts, and to create and convey mood, emotion, depth and the illusion of space.

It is useful to analyse colour in terms of:

* primary colours – yellow, red and blue.
* secondary colours, made by mixing the primary colours – orange (yellow + red), violet (red + blue) and green (blue + yellow).
* tertiary colours, made by mixing a primary colour with a secondary colour – yellow-orange (yellow + orange), red-orange (red + orange), red-violet (red + violet), blue-violet (blue + violet), blue-green (blue + green) and yellow-green (yellow + green).
* complementary colours, which are opposite each other on the colour wheel and give the greatest contrasts when used together – yellow and violet, red and green, and blue and orange.
* analogous colours, which are three colours that sit side by side on the colour wheel and when used together form a harmonious colour scheme.
* tints, which are created by adding white to a colour.
* shades, which are created by adding black to a colour.
* temperature – colours can be described as being hot/warm or cold/cool.

Immersing yourself in colour will teach you about its limitless combinations and distinctions. The more you play, the more expansive and confident your colour vocabulary will become.

colours: yellow / yellow orange / orange / orange/ red / red violet... heat + memories of India

warm colours: yellow / yellow orange / orange/ red / red violet... heat + memories of India...

cool colours: yellow green / green/ blue / blue violet / violet

Above and opposite page, left:
Colour Sketchbook (Julia Triston).
Hot and cold colours explored in
paper collages, stitch experiments
and fabric swatches.

Line

A line has a beginning and an end. It is the continuous movement of a point across a surface. Line is used to define shapes, contours and outlines. Horizontal and vertical lines convey stability, whereas diagonal lines can suggest a dynamic sense of movement. It is useful to think about line in terms of:

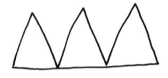

LINE

- type: straight, angular, dotted, broken, thin, thick, interrupted, wavy, long, short, continuous, tapering and intersecting.
- direction: horizontal, vertical, diagonal, spiral, curved, parallel and perpendicular.
- texture: smooth, rough, soft, hard and spiky.

SHAPE

Consciously using line will enable you to create movement, express feeling and emotion, and link areas of focus within your work. Lines don't always have to be directly drawn or stitched; they can be implied by the creative use of shapes, shadows and spaces.

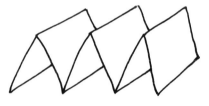

FORM

Right: **Line Exploration** (Pauline Twyman). Playing with spacing, tones and pressures with pencil.

Above: **Beauty Sketchbook** (Rachel Lombard). Developing linear samples through drawing, mark-making and stitch using paper and fabric. Left: **Dress Drawings** (Julia Triston). From left to right: observational drawing; 'taking a line for a walk' without looking at the source; exploring line details – pen on paper (see exercises, page 53).

Shape

A shape is a self-contained area enclosed by lines. It is two-dimensional (that is, flat), with height, width and area, but no depth. When a shape is drawn or placed on a background it creates a positive subject; the empty background around the positive subject is called the negative space. Good design will always make use of both positive and negative spaces.

It can be useful to consider shapes in terms of their:

- characteristics – geometric and architectural (for example, circles, squares, triangles, hexagons, arches); organic and natural (for example, petals, leaves, fish scales, cloud shapes, animal skins).
- contrasting properties – static/dynamic, restful/active, stable/unstable and solid/fluid.

A single shape or motif can be repeated to create pattern. Patterns can be developed through rotation, symmetry and tessellation. Pattern is a fundamental aspect of stitched and printed textile design, appearing in borders, edges, backgrounds, insertions and embellishments. An awareness of shape is a necessary factor in the creation of individual decorative designs.

Above: **Elephant Sketchbook** (Julia Triston). Pattern development from repeated shapes.
Above right: **Beauty Sketchbook** (Rachel Lombard). Tattoo shapes explored in waxed, bonded and stitched tissue papers.
Right: **Mermaid Mirror Sketchbook** (Rachel Lombard). Isolated shape to be used as a decorative motif. The finished item is shown on page 119.

Form

A form is a three-dimensional object, with height, width and depth. It can be viewed from many different angles, can have an inside and an outside, and can be solid or hollow. The properties of weight, scale, mass and volume can be considered within this design element.

It is useful to appreciate the contrasts that a form offers in terms of its:

- scale – is it portable or immovable, large or small?
- function – is it decorative, useful, sculptural, wearable or fit for its intended purpose?
- durability – is it permanent or temporary; can it grow and change?
- interaction – can it be turned inside out or moved around; can you walk inside or around it?
- structure – is it lacy and open, or closed and dense?

It is important to consider using the design element of form because textiles can be readily moulded, constructed, manipulated and sculpted to create three-dimensional pieces – for example, bags, boxes, hats, books, shoes and vessels.

Texture

Texture is about the quality of a surface. Everything you touch has a texture. There are two types of texture: actual (or tactile) and visual (or implied). Actual texture is what we can feel when touching a surface or an object – for example, when we run our hands over the bark of a tree. Visual texture is suggested; it is portrayed to look like it would feel – for example, a rubbing taken of tree bark looks textured, but feels flat. It is useful to define texture in terms of:

- hard: a surface that is unyielding when touched (for example, glass, ceramics, metal, wood, Bakelite).
- soft: a surface that yields when touched (for example, feathers, fur, fleece, wool, wadding).
- rough: a surface that is coarse, bumpy and irregular (for example, coconut husk, sandpaper, driftwood, brickwork, savoy cabbage leaves).
- smooth: a surface that is even and regular (for example, conker, glossy magazine paper, varnished wood, still water).
- matt: a surface that is non-reflective (for example, cork, cotton wool, newspaper, felt, bread).
- shiny: a surface that is light-reflective (for example, gemstones, polished leather, aluminium foil, mirror glass, glazed cotton).

A textured surface is not necessarily always raised; it can incorporate many different qualities. The nature of light can completely change the appearance of surfaces. Strong, bright light can create shadows that accentuate texture, whereas more diffused light can flatten, and sometimes remove, textural contrasts.

Below: **Lion Sketchbook** (Rachel Lombard). Dense textures created with plaster, threads, dripped candle wax and plastics.

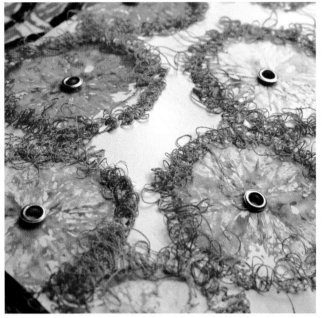

Above left: **Texture Sketchbook** (Julia Triston). Prints from lemons with eyelets and stitch. Above right: **Texture Sketchbook** (Catherine Gowthorpe). Wax crayon rubbings of fern leaves. Left: **Collection of textures** Different textured surfaces gathered from around the home.

A framework for composition

Once you have a basic understanding of these five formal elements of design you have a framework that you can use to analyse and interpret any source material or artwork. Every artist will consider the formal elements in the creation of their work, but will often use one element in particular to emphasize the intentions and concepts behind their work.

When viewing artwork in magazines, books or galleries, get into the habit of studying the overall composition and then breaking it down to identify the formal elements of design that feature in it. Consider how each formal element has been used by the artist and which one, if any, dominates.

Understanding and using the formal elements of design at these early stages will enable you to make positive choices about the development of your ideas, which will lead you to a more considered and successful outcome.

Above left: **Time and Tide Bag** (Rachel Lombard). Manipulated velvet with couching, hand stitch and embellishments. The emphasis is on texture. Above: **Brown Paper Bag** (Rachel Lombard). Paper, appliqué and padding techniques with rich, metallic machine stitch. The emphasis is on shape. Right: **Quirky Face 1** (Julia Triston). Free machine embroidery, hand stitch and embellishments on bonded silks and sweet wrappers. The emphasis is on colour.

Left: **Cosmic Towers** (Ros Murphy). Calico coated with emulsion and silk fibres and coloured with dye, perforated with a needle on the sewing machine. The emphasis is on form. Below: **Linear Landscape** (Rachel Lombard). Silk-painted cotton, hand stitch and button detail. The emphasis is on line.

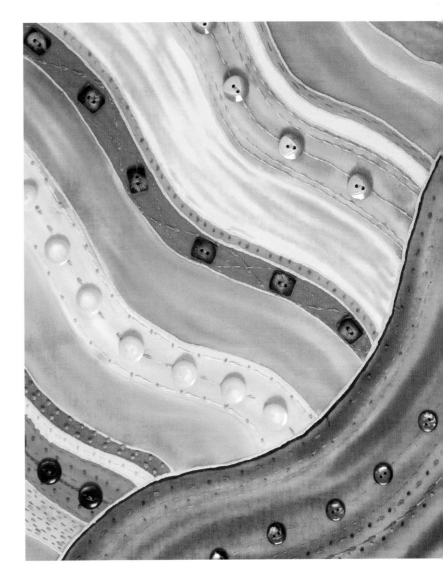

Right: Photographs of primary sources demonstrating the formal design elements in our everyday surroundings. Columns from left to right: Colour, Line, Shape, Form and Texture.

Chapter 4

DESIGN DEVELOPMENT

tools, equipment and materials to explore

developing a design

printing

resists

photocopying and scanning

collage

conclusion to Part 2

Left: **Sweetie Face** (Julia Triston). Collage of sweet wrappers on a painted and stitched page, from the Faces sketchbook shown on page 54.

In Chapter 3 we looked at how to begin the visual exploration of your source material and to consider the formal elements of design. The aim of this chapter is to encourage you to move away from a basic and literal interpretation of your sources towards a more abstract one, and to work spontaneously to capture the essence and details of your sources. We will show you different ways to develop and expand your responses, enabling you to move from a representational interpretation of your source material to a more imaginative and creative one. This will ultimately lead to a visually stimulating and rewarding resolved textile piece.

Tools, equipment and materials to explore

Taking your work on to the next stage will involve an investment in some basic art and design tools, equipment and materials. These don't need to be expensive, complicated or difficult to source – in fact, many useful implements can be found around the home.

Tools and equipment

You will be able to source useful tools and equipment from every room in your house. The table below shows some examples.

KITCHEN	GARAGE	BATHROOM	OFFICE
iron	soldering iron	hairdryer	stapler
potato masher	glue gun	nail scissors	hole punch
scissors	paintbrushes	tweezers	computer
chopping board	pliers	toothbrushes	printer/
pastry brushes	sandpaper	old shower curtain	scanner
cutlery	picture frames and	hair straighteners	photocopier
scourers and	spare glass	brushes	ruler
sponges	plastic sheeting	combs	laminator
measuring jugs	craft knife	nail brush	guillotine

Left: **Sweetie Face**
(Julia Triston). Shown in
full on page 46.

Materials

Around your home you will find a wealth of useful everyday materials – from packaging to toiletries – that can be used in both design and stitch work. The table below shows some examples.

KITCHEN	GARAGE	BATHROOM	OFFICE
polystyrene trays	washers	nail varnish	staples
ring pulls	tins of paint	cotton buds (swabs)	glue
cocktail sticks	screws and nails	make-up	masking tape
food colouring	candles	blister packs	double-sided tape
spices	tile spacers	combs	sticky tape
tea and coffee	pegs	old towels	parcel tape
baking parchment	liquid boot polish	cosmetic sponges	erasers
cling film	carpet underlay	soap bar scraps	pens and pencils
vegetable and fruit	Polyfilla filler powder	loofah	old CDs
netting	string	body scourers	spray mount
corks	duct tape	cotton wool	labels
doilies	pipe cleaners	toothpaste lids	sticky Velcro
ice cream and	wallpaper paste	corn plasters	bubble wrap
margarine tubs	old net curtains	bleach	paper fasteners
plastic bags	fuse wires	emery boards	paperclips
sea salt	varnishes and stains	contact lens cases	treasury tags
spatulas	spray paint	false nails	elastic bands
drinking straws	plastic plant labels	empty plastic bottles	old computer parts
bottle lids and tops	brushes	shower caps	old pen nibs and lids
kebab sticks	cable ties	dental floss	bulldog clips

Below: **Neck Ruff** (Mary-Anne Morrison). Pleated flock organza with machine-stitched edges and ends.

As well as lots of readily accessible items found around the home, there are some things that we suggest you invest in:

- papers and sketchbooks
- artists' paintbrushes
- wax crayons
- acrylic paints
- inks
- silk paints
- Brusho
- Markal Paintstiks
- chalk pastels
- oil pastels
- gutta

PAPER

There are many different types of specialist papers on the market that can be used in your design work, such as Japanese fibre papers, Khadi paper, abaca tissue and watercolour paper. Although these are lovely to use, they can be expensive, and simpler and cheaper alternatives can be found around the home, such as:

- photocopier paper
- graph paper
- wrapping paper
- newspaper
- magazines
- old books
- paper cake cases
- doilies
- tissue paper
- Yellow Pages
- old envelopes
- brown paper
- tracing paper
- greaseproof paper (alternative to tracing paper)
- lining paper
- wallpaper

Below: A selection of papers, including newsprint and handmade paper (Sandra Meech).

It is not always easy being faced with a blank sheet of paper at the start of every project or process. Creating a pile of decorated backgrounds and surfaces to work on at a later date can be rewarding and useful. Papers can be coloured, sponged, spattered, rollered, stained or sprayed. They can also be altered and textured by wetting, stretching, crumpling, weaving, tearing, layering and collaging.

Right: A selection of dyed, painted and decorated papers (Sandra Meech).

Developing a design

Design development is an essential stage in the process of creating your project. It will take time to develop a design that works, and to create one that you are happy with. It is important that you do not rush this stage, but allow your design work time to *evolve*. This is not a linear process – you can revisit and rework different parts of your design and artwork at any stage of development. Allow yourself the freedom to explore and experiment with different techniques and materials, and you may well find that the process of developing your design takes you in unexpected and exciting directions.

Mark-making

When interpreting your source material, try to capture the *essence* of your collection, rather than drawing precisely what you see. Thinking about making a mark on a background can be less intimidating than thinking about 'drawing'. Aim to make marks that convey a personal interpretation of your source material, rather than detailed representational drawings. The strength and direction of a mark or line can convey a mood or feeling. For example, a heavy zigzag line can suggest turbulence and instability, whereas a smoother, softer horizontal line can express a sense of calm and peace.

Marks can be made with many items that can be found around you. Tools, equipment and materials from your kitchen, garage, bathroom and office, as mentioned in the tables on pages 48 and 49, can also be used to produce exciting effects and unusual results.

Right: Experimental mark-making with pens, pencils, paints, charcoal and crayons (Julia Triston, Rachel Lombard).

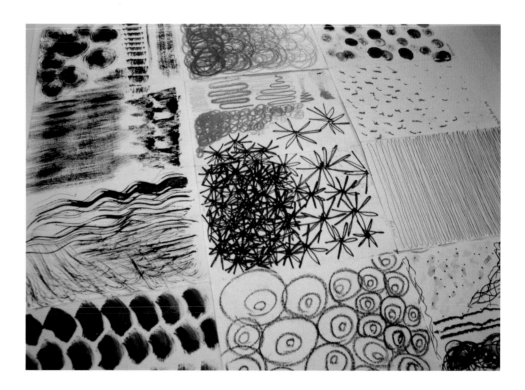

Drawing for design

Referring to your source material and associated sketches or photographs, study the surfaces, outlines and silhouettes, picking out details that can be developed into simple designs and focusing on the element of line. In your sketchbook, draw these details as freely as you can across your pages, experimenting with a variety of pens, pencils, crayons, pastels, etc. If you find this difficult, and many people do, you could try:

- drawing with your 'other' hand.
- drawing with your sketching hand covered while looking at your source.
- 'taking a line for a walk' – that is, not taking your pencil or pen off the page until you have completed your drawing.
- drawing in pen, so that you cannot rub out.
- wetting your page before you start to draw with a non-permanent fine liner or felt-tip pen, so that your lines 'bleed' as you draw them.
- using a thick marker pen to create a different type of line.

These 'free drawings' can be used as a starting point for further stages of the design development process.

Right: Observational drawing, mark-making and paper modelling from primary source material (Maggie Smith).

Printing

Printing is a great way to decorate papers and fabric. Simple repeat designs or complex patterns can be built up in layers of colours and tones. Areas of texture can be quickly created across your surfaces. It might be possible to print directly with your gathered materials (for example, a potato masher or a loofah), but if not, there are many different ways of printing designs on to your background paper or fabric, some of which are explored in this section.

Block printing

Blocks can be bought ready-made, but it is much more exciting to make your own, as you are in control when it comes to determining its size, shape and complexity. The easiest block to begin with is a square, as this can be repeated and rotated to build a pattern that will fit together in continuous strips and blocks to cover a surface.

To get an interesting design for your print block, cut out a square window of about 4cm (1½in) from a piece of plain card and lay this over your line drawings in order to isolate a small area that you can interpret into print. Look for linear patterns or very simple shapes – move your window across your drawing, changing the angle to find unusual details as you do so. Any design that you develop will be more effective if it is asymmetrical. Use your window to mark out a few square boxes in your sketchbook and draw your isolated patterns and shapes into these squares. Play with several designs, colouring them in to indicate possible positive and negative areas – that is, the areas that are to be raised and the sunken spaces in between. When you make your print block, remember that the printed image will be in reverse.

Left: **Faces Sketchbook** (Julia Triston). Developing pattern possibilities from an isolated shape, examining positive and negative spaces.

MAKING A SIMPLE PRINT BLOCK

There are several cheap and easy ways to create a simple print block:

Carving into a surface with a sharp knife or point, for example:
- a potato – which is quick and cheap, but not permanent
- a pencil eraser – a longer-lasting alternative
- thin polystyrene tile or packaging

Cutting shapes and applying them to thick card, for example:
- gluing card on to card
- sticking coloured foam shapes on to card with double-sided tape

Applying items to a firm surface, for example:
- string lines held in place with double-sided tape
- glue gun 'doodles' applied directly on to the print block surface
- thick lace held in place with glue

Note that some blocks will have a longer life span if you coat them with varnish or PVA glue before initial use.

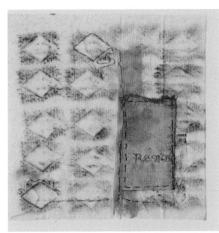

Top: **Print Blocks** (Rachel Lombard, Julia Triston). Handmade from foam, potato, card, polystyrene, string, corn plasters, eraser and glue-gun doodles. Above: **Print sample** (Cas Holmes). Biscuit print on wet wipe with appliqué.

MEDIUMS FOR BLOCK PRINTING

Acrylic paints, poster paints and printing inks come in a wide range of colours and a variety of finishes, including metallic, pearlized, neon and iridescent. Household emulsion tester pots are readily available and can make a good cheap alternative. Other less obvious mediums to experiment with include gutta, coloured varnishes, commercial ink pads, and even liquid shoe polish with a sponge applicator. There are many other commercial products on the market – for example, texture gels, fabric paints and Xpandaprint – that can produce interesting effects.

The chosen medium can be applied directly to the print block in a variety of ways – for example, with a sponge, paintbrush, roller or a cloth. Each method will give a slightly different texture to the printed surface.

USING BLOCK PRINTING CREATIVELY

Here are some ideas that you can experiment with to achieve successful results with your block printing:

- choose colours and background papers and fabrics that reflect the colours and textures in your source materials, remembering to consider analagous and complementary colour combinations.
- change the direction of the block in regular and irregular ways to create new patterns, designs and motifs.
- print with the block in a horizontal line until the print medium fades – tonal lines will emerge – then reload the block and repeat the process.
- print the same block, with a different colour or rotation, on top of your previous printed surface to layer your design – this builds colour and texture.
- experiment with painting sections of the print block different colours to create pattern within pattern.
- print with one block on top of another – this overlaying can be very effective.
- once the printing is dry, apply a wash of colour over your printed surface – this can produce interesting and surprising results (ink and Brusho are ideal for this).
- bleach can be used to make a mark over the top of a washed ink or Brusho surface. Before you work with bleach, please read the health and safety information on page 121.

It is important to keep all the print blocks and printed surfaces you produce, including the ones you are not happy with. Everything will have a direct relevance to your source material and may well come in useful at other stages and with other processes.

Right: **Elephant Sketchbook** (Julia Triston). Block printing with acrylic paint from carved potatoes, with different rotations, on to various papers.

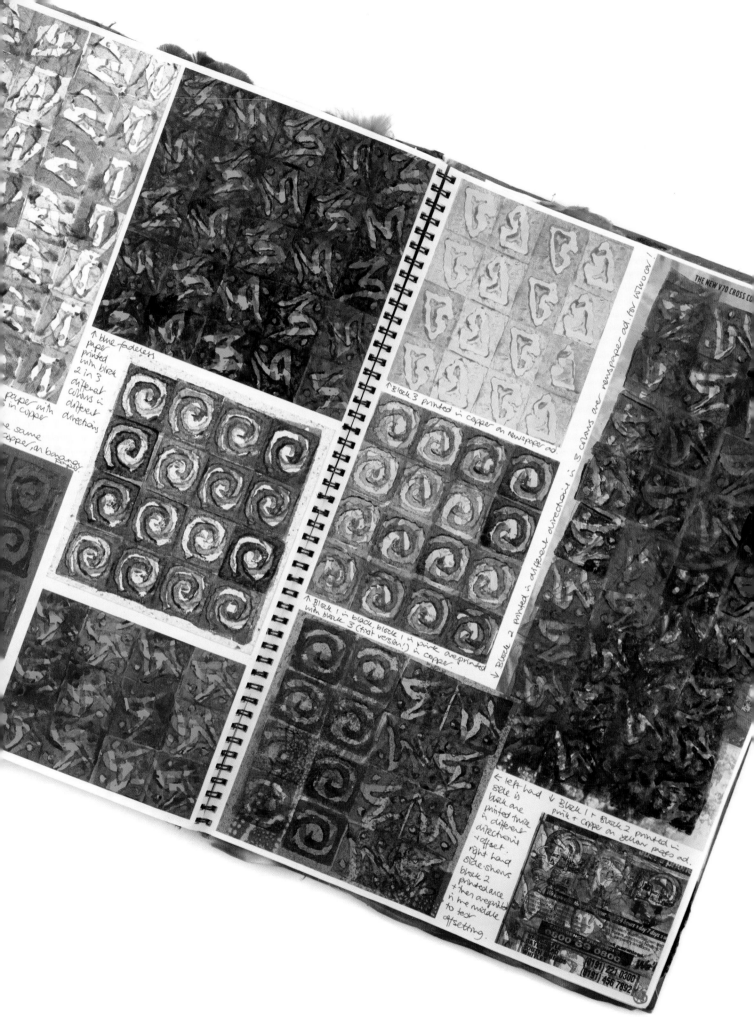

↑ blue faders paper printed with block 2 in 3 different colours in different directions

paper with in copper

same copper in banana paper

↑ Block 3 printed in copper on newspaper ad.

← Block 2 printed in different directions in 3 colours are newspaper ad for Volvo car!

↑ Block 1 in black, block 1 in pink are printed with block 3 (that version) in copper.

← Block 2 printed in different directions is

← left hand side is block are printed twice in different directions + offset. right hand side shows block 2 printed once + then are printed in the middle to tear offsetting.

↓ Block 1 + Block 2 printed in pink + copper on yellow pages ad.

Monoprinting

This printing process can produce spontaneous and exciting results. Paint is applied to a non-porous surface, such as a sheet of glass, plastic or acetate, and drawn into to create a design. Paper or fabric is then pressed against the painted surface to produce a print. As the name suggests, each time a print is made it is unique and therefore unrepeatable. Monoprinting is a great technique for taking a step away from a literal interpretation of your source material because you cannot predict or completely control the results. You can focus on line, shape or colour and the process can produce interesting textures.

Your printing surface needs to be flat and smooth – a piece of glass from an old picture frame is ideal (but be sure to protect yourself by covering the sharp edges with tape before use). A square of old vinyl flooring, a plastic tablemat or a sheet of plastic taped to your work surface will also work.

MEDIUMS FOR MONOPRINTING

There are many products that can be used for monoprinting. Commercial printing inks are ideal for the purpose, but often come in large quantities and can be expensive. Acrylic paints are a readily available and inexpensive medium, although they may need diluting (with water, a water-based varnish, PVA glue or wallpaper paste) as they can dry out very quickly.

Paint can be applied to the glass or plastic sheet with a number of different tools – for example, a roller, paintbrush, sponge or spatula. Each tool will create a different texture.

USING MONOPRINTING CREATIVELY

We have found that the following methods produce interesting results when monoprinting:

Before taking your print, mark or draw into the painted glass or plastic sheet. Different implements will produce a different quality of mark. Consider using:
- cotton buds (swabs)
- edges of an old credit card
- bubble wrap
- old toothbrush
- fingers
- paintbrush
- source materials (for example, a shell or twig)
- comb

Roll out a very thin layer of paint on your printing plate. Lay your paper or fabric on top, and draw on to the back of it before taking it off the print plate. Try using:
- pen or pencil
- end of a paintbrush
- fingers
- fork

Mask out areas on your painted print plate before taking a print. Experiment with:

- torn or cut paper shapes (refer to your source material for inspiration)
- leaves, ferns and petals
- threads
- scrim or lace

Remove areas of paint before printing by pressing an object on to the painted print plate – it will remove some of the paint and leave a negative impression. Try using:

- items from your collection of source materials
- print blocks
- lace or paper doilies
- a piece of cloth to rub out areas

Opposite page and below: **Monoprinting, Time and Tide Sketchbook** (Rachel Lombard). Acrylic paint mixed with water-based varnish and washed with Brusho when dry.

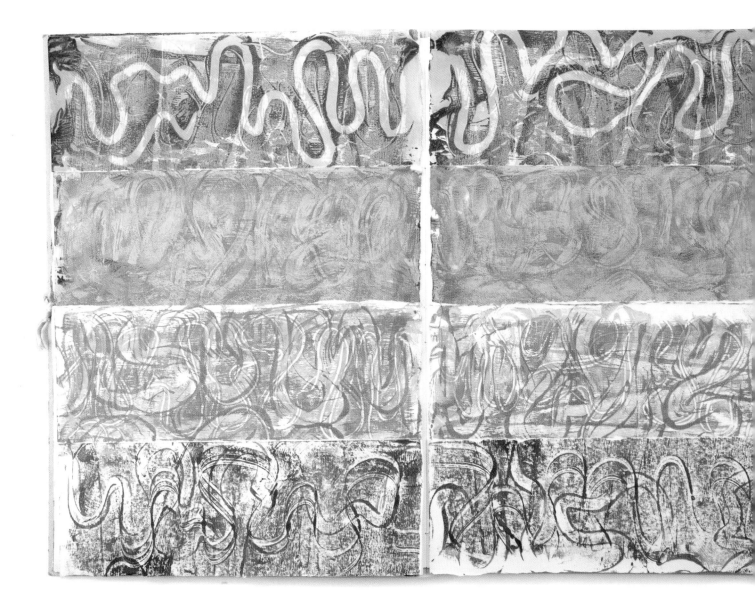

Resists

A resist is anything that will prevent ink, paint or dye penetrating a surface. Traditional resist techniques on fabric include tie-dye, batik and shibori, where areas of the fabric are tied, waxed or bound in patterns before dyeing, to maintain the original colour of the background fabric.

Resist techniques provide a wonderful opportunity to build layers of colour and pattern on paper as well as fabric. Used creatively, resist techniques can be a valuable tool in developing your designs.

Below: **Masking Out sample** (Julia Triston). Silver paint sprayed through lace, which acts as a resist (lace and resist on paper both shown). Opposite page: **Tie-dye with Stitch Resist** (Karen Randles). Indigo-dyed and waxed turban cotton samples with hand stitch and button embellishment.

Tie-dye

A resist pattern can be created on fabric by holding folds, tucks, pleats and gathers in place with stitch, bulldog clips, pegs, string or elastic bands. Objects such as pebbles and coins can be tied around and bound tightly into the fabric. The tied fabric is then plunged into and soaked in a dye bath, which can be as simple as an old bucket or saucepan. Follow the manufacturer's instructions carefully when mixing up and fixing dyes.

Once the fabric has been dyed the resists can be removed and the pattern revealed. Resists can be added or removed between dye baths, and layers of colour can be built up, starting with your pale colours. Remember your colour-mixing theory when building up layers of colour – if you first dye with yellow and then add blue, your end result will be green.

Masking out

A resist can also be directly applied to a surface and then painted or spray-painted over. Areas of a fabric or paper background can be masked with:

- masking tape
- masking fluid
- stencils
- found objects

These masks can be removed and reapplied in new positions. More colour can then be worked over the surface, so that layers of shapes and patterns are created.

Wax

Wax is a versatile medium that can be used to create resists on paper and fabric. There are traditional and specialist methods that require specific tools and equipment, but simple wax crayons and household candles can be used creatively to further the development of your designs for stitch.

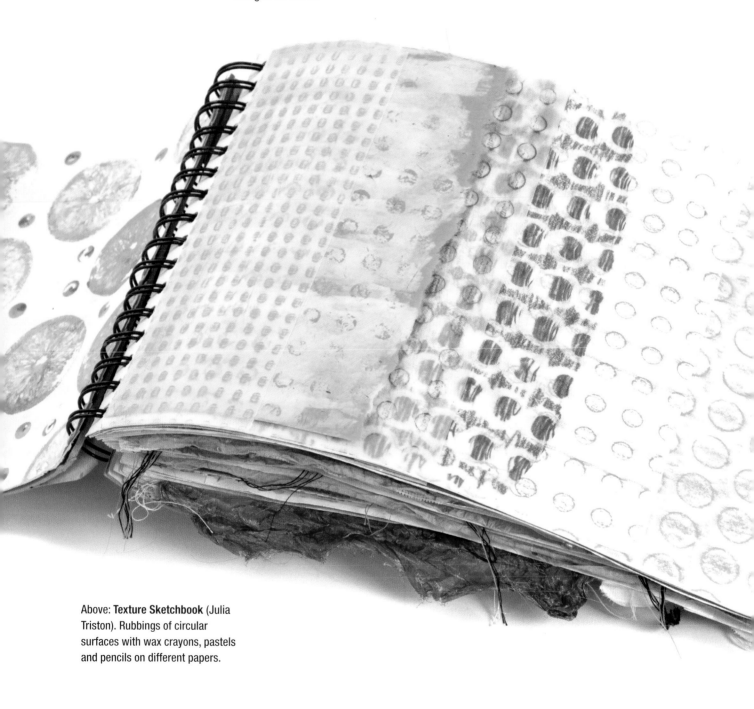

Above: **Texture Sketchbook** (Julia Triston). Rubbings of circular surfaces with wax crayons, pastels and pencils on different papers.

HOT WAX AND BATIK

Traditionally, batik is a resist process in which hot wax is applied to a fabric with a special tool called a *tjanting* (these, along with wax pots and batik wax, can be bought from a specialist supplier). The fabric is then painted over or immersed in cold-water dyes. Once the dye has dried, more wax can be applied to the surface to mask out areas of the new background colour. Layers of wax, then more dye, can be built up to create a complex shaded design. When the piece is complete, the wax can be removed to reveal the areas where it has resisted the dye and the pattern has formed. Solid areas of wax can be broken up by crumpling the waxed fabric before the dyeing process – dye will penetrate the broken wax and a distinctive 'crackle effect' is created. Most of the batik wax can be removed from fabric by ironing it between sheets of newsprint paper – be careful to protect your ironing surface.

Above: **Elephant Batik** (Julia Triston). Resist with hot wax on cotton fabric, painted with silk paints. 35 x 24cm (13¾ x 9½in).

Hot wax can also be applied to fabric or paper with an old paintbrush and other implements, such as cutlery, a potato masher or a cork. Instead of using dye, a wash of Brusho can be used over waxed designs on paper.

COLD WAX AND RUBBINGS

Wax crayons and household candles can be used to create a rubbing when scribbled on paper held in place over a textured surface. There are many interesting surfaces around you that can be used for this technique – for example, an old chopping board, a woven basket, tree bark, a piece of lace or a paving stone. Look back through your source material to see what textures you can take a rubbing from.

This technique is a quick way of 'drawing' to record your surroundings. Simple rubbings can be made more interesting by layering one coloured wax over another to build colour and pattern.

Wax rubbings can often be enhanced by applying a wash of colour over the top – Brusho colours and inks are ideal for this sort of colour wash. This resist method is a way of quickly building visual texture.

Rubbings can be taken with a variety of other mediums, but not all will take an overlaid wash. Experiment with the following and see what works best for you:

- oil pastels
- chalk pastels
- coloured pencils
- graphite sticks
- Markal Paintstiks

Photocopying and scanning

A photocopier and scanner are useful tools for creating multiple images from a single source. To achieve a crisp copy, sources have to be relatively flat, but they can be real objects, not just secondary sources from books and magazines – for example, you could try photocopying leaves, items of clothing, doilies or threads.

Once scanned, images can be manipulated – enlarged, reduced, mirrored, rotated, darkened, lightened, etc. – to give a new perspective on your source material. Colour can be added, removed or altered to change the balance of the composition completely. Images can be printed on cheap copier paper to cut down design costs.

Your copied images can be worked into, and enhanced, by:

- colouring in
- washing colour over
- tearing, cutting or scoring into
- repiecing
- cutting into patterns and borders
- layering
- weaving
- rolling into cylinders
- folding into origami forms
- crumpling
- pleating
- stitching into
- tracing from

Each of these ideas can take you a step away from your source material. You can rescan, rephotocopy or photograph your experiments at any time throughout this process. This can lead to unexpected and inspiring results that may move your work on in a new direction.

Right: Experimental 3-D design source photocopied and sketched (Rachel Lombard).

Collage

A collage is a montage of different things – for example, fabrics, text, rubbings, printed surfaces, photocopies, photographs and collected objects – that are stuck down to create a cohesive themed composition. A collage can:

- link and connect aspects of research
- gather together disparate elements to create a narrative
- progress an idea or develop a technique
- define a focus for design development work

This technique is also a visual tool, which can bring together a myriad of sources, ideas or materials that make some form of sense without the need for notes and explanation. A collage can be two- or three-dimensional, and itself may be used for a rubbing, photocopied, scanned or photographed, or drawn or stitched into to further your design work.

When developing your own designs, consider whether there are certain themes within your source material and ongoing design work that can be brought together visually through a collage – for example, colours and textures.

Conclusion to Part 2

In Part 2 we have examined many accessible ways of capturing the essence and details of your source materials by creating designs for stitch. Not all these techniques will be applicable to your source material, nor will all your experiments be successful. However, it is important to keep all the experimental work you produce, as even your less successful outcomes can teach you lessons or be reworked.

Techniques can be combined – for example, a monoprinted background could have a texture rubbed over the top, or a rubbing could be colour-washed and then overprinted. But be careful – combining too many techniques within the same piece can lead to design work that is busy and unfocused. Keep referring to the formal elements of design and use them as a framework to review the progress of your development work.

Right: **Beauty Sketchbook** (Rachel Lombard). Collage of glossy magazine papers with machine stitch, focusing on the search for perfection through the use of cosmetic enhancement.

PART 3 : MOVING ON TO STITCH

Chapter 5

IDEAS AND POSSIBILITIES, SAMPLES AND EXPERIMENTS

selecting tools and materials

selecting fabrics

selecting threads

hand stitching

machine stitching

using hand and machine stitch creatively

fabric manipulation

layering and piecing

appliqué

edges

embellishments

conclusion to Part 3

Left: **Chain stitch sampler** (Vicky Hutchinson). Experimental hand stitching to explore size, style, tension, shape and direction of stitch.

In this chapter we will look at ways to take your design development work forward into stitch, and give you the tools to enable you to develop a series of creative, relevant and useful samples based on your ideas and their possibilities. Continuing to keep the design elements of colour, line, shape, form and texture at the forefront of your mind will provide you with a framework through which to examine your source materials.

Recording your findings and learning points in your sketchbook will give you an insight into where you have come from, an understanding of where you are now, and can help to clarify where your work is going.

Selecting tools and materials

A basic sewing kit is a requirement for all stitching, and you can add to it as your experience grows and your projects become more complex. To begin with, your sewing kit should include:

- needles – there are many different types for different fabrics and threads; our favourites are chenille needles, which have a sharp point and large eye, and tapestry needles with a blunt point and large eye.
- pins – there are many varieties available on the market. Whichever you choose, make sure they are sharp.
- scissors – choose a small, sharp, pointed pair for snipping threads, and a large sharp pair for cutting fabrics (keep your kitchen scissors for cutting paper).
- threads – polyester cottons are strong and come in many colours for basic construction work and for stitching on embellishments, etc.
- hoop – a round wooden 20cm (8in) hoop is vital for some machine embroidery techniques and traditional hand stitching, as it keeps the surface of the fabric taut while it is being stitched (note that binding the inside ring will help to hold the fabric firmly in place and minimize marking).
- tape measure – one with both metric and imperial measurements is handy.
- thimble – the use of a thimble is an acquired taste: some people never stitch without them, others never use them.
- carbon paper – this is useful for transferring designs on to fabric.
- tailor's chalk – this is a valuable tool for marking out lines or areas to stitch or join on your piece of fabric.

Selecting fabrics

There are hundreds of fabrics on the market to choose from; they can be plain, patterned, textured, shot, thick, thin, shiny, matt, printed, stretchy, furry or transparent. Some are much more common and suitable for stitch than others, and some are specialist and have a very specific purpose, such as materials used for dance costumes. Fabrics can be bought by the metre, but many shops will sell 10cm (4in) strips, which can be useful for sampling purposes or small projects. Recycled clothing and household linen can also be a great resource for textile work.

The table below outlines some common and some more specialist fabrics used in hand and machine embroidery, as well as some alternative and recycled 'fabrics' that you could use in innovative and experimental ways.

COMMON FABRICS	SPECIALIST FABRICS	ALTERNATIVE/RECYCLED 'FABRICS'
calico	pelmet Vilene (Pellon)	vegetable and fruit netting
plain cotton	buckram	cellophane
linen	sinamay	florists' paper
denim	polar fleece	sweet wrappers
felt	fun furs	plastic packaging
scrim	tulle	bubble wrap
muslin	Tyvek	foils
velvet	Lycra	papers
organdie	Lutradur	abaca tissue
organza	coir	silk carrier rods
corduroy	bridal fabrics	metal shims
chiffon	leather and suede	carpet underlay
silk	leatherette	plant leaves
taffeta	Angelina fibres	bandages
satin	furnishing fabrics	carrier bags
polyester	Lurex	cotton wool
polycotton	jute scrim	fibre papers
voile	towelling	potato sacks
tweed	lace	paper money
counted thread fabrics	silk viscose velvet	tea bags
canvases	tissue silk	corrugated cardboard
dissolvable fabrics	hessian	wireform
nylon	jersey	body scourers
poplin	knitted fabrics	kitchen towels
gingham	coloured foam sheets	plastic files
interfacing	tights	flock wallpaper

Above: Collection of common, specialist and alternative/recycled fabrics.

Selecting threads

For both hand and machine stitching there is a wealth of 'threads' on the market to choose from. Some are for a very specific purpose, such as Japanese gold threads for goldwork, and some are very versatile, such as stranded cottons for counted thread work. Threads can be thick, thin, metallic, shiny, matt, smooth, fluffy, plain, dyed, variegated, stranded, twisted, knobbly, textured, fine, coarse, natural, synthetic, knitted or hollow. They can be bought singly or in multi-packs, on cones or reels, in hanks or balls, in skeins or by the metre. You can make your own threads by tearing or cutting fabric into thin strips, plaiting or twisting thin threads together to create thicker ones, or zigzagging over several threads with the sewing machine.

The table below shows the range of traditional, more specialist and contemporary 'threads' available.

TRADITIONAL THREADS	SPECIALIST THREADS	CONTEMPORARY 'THREADS'
stranded cottons	crochet cottons	string
coton à broder	machine embroidery threads	dental floss
silks	buttonhole threads	lace
perle cotton	Nymo (beading thread)	raffia
cotton machine threads	crewel wools	garden twine
polyester tacking threads	lamé (stranded metallic)	paper string
soft embroidery threads	water-soluble threads	packing tapes
fine/medium cottons	gimp	thin strips of fabric
quilting threads	underthreads (pre-wound	shoelaces
chenille	machine bobbin)	cassette tape
knitting yarns	milliner's wire	plastic-coated wire
bouclé	Marlitt (stranded viscose)	grasses
elastic	wool roving	strips of carrier bags
viscose/rayon ribbons	metal threads (Japanese	fishing line
fine ribbon	threads, purls, etc., for	pipe cleaners
linen threads	goldwork)	fine wires
floss	fine leather strips	hair

Right: Collection of traditional, specialist and contemporary threads for hand and machine stitch.

Hand stitching

A stitch is a way of making a mark on fabric with thread. It is an extension of the marks you have been making on paper in your design work, but with different mediums that have different properties. Every stitch can be identified by its own individual structure and rhythm, giving it a distinctive pattern and texture when repeatedly stitched across a surface.

In a traditional style of embroidery stitches are expected to be regular, even, uniform, precise, neat and tidy. Stitches are often categorized into groups for different purposes – for example, running stitch and chain stitch are used as 'outline' stitches, whereas bullion and French knots are used as 'isolated and texture' stitches. Stitches that we have enjoyed using in our work include running stitch, couching, fly stitch, twisted chain, raised chain band, buttonhole stitch, Pekinese stitch, spider's web and woven web, straight stitch, seeding, French knots.

Stitches can also be used more freely as marks across a surface to create a more contemporary embroidered textile. It is possible to maintain the individual structure and rhythm of a stitch and play around with its tension, size, pattern, proportion and scale. This is a way of exploring a stitch to discover the patterns, shapes, lines and individual marks it can make. Focusing on a particular stitch will enable you to experiment, break with tradition, and push your chosen stitch to its extremes.

Exploring hand stitch

Refer to your design development work and think about what marks, lines and textures could be directly translated into stitch marks. When exploring the possibilities of an individual stitch in a sampler, or when interpreting your designs, you can make exciting and innovative discoveries. Your stitches or lines of stitch could be any of those listed in the table below.

straight	horizontal	vertical	mirrored	symmetrical
zigzagged	meandering	undulating	curved	swirled
circular	spiralling	radiating	looped	crisscrossed
twisted	whipped	knotted	layered	overlaid
regular	irregular	loose	tight	angular
double	single	threaded	couched	haphazard
blended	manipulated	distressed	echoed	lumpy
textured	embellished	stretched	wrapped	flowing
integrated	rough	smooth	scattered	woven
graduated	exploded	deep	solid	interlocked
interrupted	diagonal	wide	narrow	uneven
long	short	dense	airy	patterned
paired	grouped	distorted	growing	vanishing
gathered	rotated	reversed	contorted	stacked
sparse	clustered	flowing	pulled	contained

When exploring stitch, your background fabric should be fairly plain, and your threads should be chosen from a limited colour palette, so that they do not compete with your stitch marks. If you choose to work with a hoop, remember to move it around on your fabric, so that you don't end up with lots of circular samples! Think creatively while stitching. Here are a few of our tips:

- your stitch marks are what is important – don't try to create a picture from your experiments.
- think of your stitch explorations as doodles in threads.
- keep turning your fabric around to view your stitching from different angles.
- the back can become the front – turn your fabric over; or you can stitch from both sides.
- try stitching off the edge of the fabric.
- distress your stitching with sandpaper or cut into it with scissors.
- stitching can be both decorative and functional – many stitches can be used to apply and couch other things to the surface.
- don't let the thickness of the thread dictate the scale of your stitching – a thick thread can be used to make small marks, and a thin thread can be used to make bigger, bolder marks.

Remember that it is important when stitching to record your experiments and ideas as you go along, so that you can repeat them at a later date.

Opposite page: **Couching Stitch Sampler** (Vicky Hutchinson). Hand stitch exploring linear patterns on striped pyjama fabric. Below left: **Buttonhole Bars** (Catherine Gowthorpe). Experimental, dense stitching to create a raised, textured surface. Bottom left: **Blanket-stitched Wheels** (Catherine Gowthorpe). Experimental stitch sample in different threads to solidly cover a background. Below right: **French Knots Sampler** (Rhona Mitchell). Densely stitched French knots on patterned fabric, inspired by lichen.

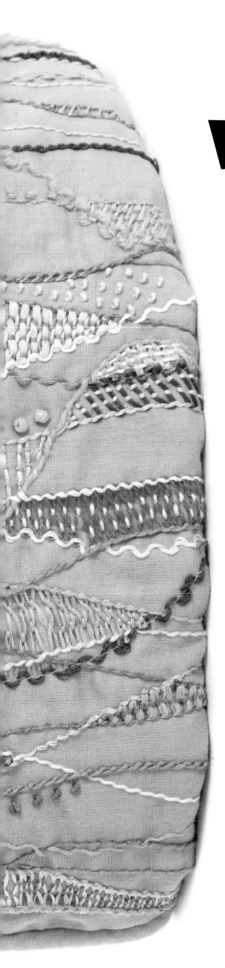

Machine stitching

You may already own a sewing machine, but perhaps have used it only for basic and household sewing. However, a sewing machine is a wonderful tool for creative stitching, and with practice you will be able to use it confidently to explore a range of techniques.

When experimenting with your sewing machine it is advisable to refer to your manufacturer's instruction manual, so that you know how to thread the top and bobbin threads correctly, change a needle, alter the top and bottom tensions, and vary the stitch length and width. For free machine embroidery it is necessary to know how to drop, or cover, the feed dog (the bottom teeth that grip the fabric beneath the needle) and change the standard foot to a darning foot (a round or horseshoe-shaped foot that allows the fabric to move freely underneath it). Sewing machines need to be taken care of – refer to your sewing machine manual for maintenance instructions and have your machine serviced regularly.

When learning to use your sewing machine creatively it is a good idea to play with some familiar stitches and use them in different ways to explore their possibilities for decorating and embellishing your fabrics.

Calico is an ideal fabric to use for your initial machine stitch experiments as it is sturdy with a firm weave, and a good-quality dressmaking thread is fine to use when you are learning the basics. There is a huge range of specialist machine threads available, including rayons, cottons, polyesters, metallics, silks and buttonhole threads. They come in a wonderful and wide range of colours, textures and finishes. Some specialist machine threads (especially metallics) are more difficult to use than others; it will be easier to stitch with them when you have become more confident with machine techniques.

Set stitches

All sewing machines will have straight and zigzag stitches. Most will also have a range of functional and decorative stitches, such as blind hem and scallops. As well as being used for their intended purposes, they can be used creatively to embellish and make marks across your fabric, build pattern and texture, and attach and apply bits and pieces to your surface.

STRAIGHT STITCH

Begin by familiarizing yourself with the basic straight stitch on your sewing machine. Start by experimenting with the following ideas and you will find that even this basic stitch can produce creative and interesting results:

- experiment with changing the tension – tightening the top tension will pucker and gather your fabric, whereas a loose tension will leave loopy, textured stitches.
- increase the stitch length – longer stitches will form a foundation that could then be woven through with hand threads.
- stitch vertical lines closely together to make solid areas of dense linear stitching.
- build patterns by crossing lines of differently coloured stitching.
- vary the thickness and finish of your threads to create texture.

ZIGZAG STITCH

Machine zigzag stitch can also be used to produce a variety of interesting lines and marks. The following ideas will produce different linear effects:

- experiment with changing the width of the stitch to produce thick and thin lines of stitching.
- alter the stitch length to make solid or more open stitched lines.
- change the setting of the width as you are stitching to form wavy, directional lines.
- stitch solid lines next to each other to build up a striped effect.
- create grids with your zigzag stitching – these could then be further embellished or filled in with hand stitch.

DECORATIVE AND FUNCTIONAL STITCHES

Pre-set and automatic stitches on the machine can offer a range of intricate and regular patterns; they can be explored and used more creatively by trying the following:

- lengthen the decorative/functional stitches to see how they stretch and change.
- broaden (if possible) the decorative/functional stitches to see how they distort.
- combine patterns to develop new ones of your own.
- use the same pattern with different threads to see how the thickness or texture changes the quality of the pattern.
- experiment with a twin needle – decorative stitches can look effective when 'echoed' with two threads (be careful that your decorative stitch width settings do not exceed the gap in your machine foot, otherwise your twin needle will break).
- overstitch one pattern on top of another to build dense, textured areas.

Opposite page: **Tea Cosy** (Catherine Gowthorpe). Cotton fabric with a foundation of straight machine stitching, woven through with hand threads. Whole piece shown on page 121.
Above: **Decorative and functional stitch sampler** (Julia Triston). Machine set patterns stitched over ribbons and painted strips of bias fabric.
Right: **Zigzag stitch sample** (Julia Triston). Experiments in both set and free zigzag stitching on the machine.

Free machine embroidery

By making a few straightforward technical adjustments, you can turn your sewing machine into a sophisticated drawing tool, opening up a whole new world of exciting and creative possibilities. Free machine embroidery is a technique that allows you to set and control the parameters of the direction, density and complexity of stitch, enabling you to 'take a line for a walk'. Anything you can draw with a pencil you can 'draw' with stitch on a machine. When drawing with a pencil the paper remains still and the pencil moves in your hand across the surface; in free machine embroidery the needle remains in one place and will stitch on the spot – a mark is created only when the fabric is moved underneath the needle.

The technique of free machine embroidery can be frustrating to master, but it is well worth persevering with – like any skill it will take time and practice to perfect.

Right: **Harlequin Face** (Julia Triston). Solid free machine embroidery on a calico base.

FREE MACHINE EMBROIDERY SETTINGS

To set up your machine successfully for free machine embroidery, you will need to:

- drop, or cover, the feed dog.
- set the stitch length to zero.
- fit a darning foot.
- use the same weight of thread on the top and bottom bobbin of your machine.
- make sure, if you have a bottom bobbin race, that your thread runs clockwise when unwinding.
- start each project with a sharp, new 90/14 needle.
- place a piece of calico in a bound 20cm (8in) embroidery hoop and pull so that the fabric is taut; if your calico is thin, use a double layer.
- fit an extension table if you have one.

STARTING TO STITCH

Once you have set up your machine for free machine embroidery, described above, you are ready to begin stitching. Follow the instructions below carefully to achieve a successful result:

- put your hoop under the needle so that the surface of the fabric is touching the base plate (you will be stitching into what would be the back of the fabric if you were hand stitching).
- move the needle down through the fabric and back up again to bring the bobbin thread through to the surface of the fabric; hold on to both ends of the top and bobbin threads for the first few stitches.
- hold the edges of the hoop securely, resting the sides of your hands on the machine's base plate – and keeping your fingers well away from the needle!
- starting with the needle in your fabric, stitch slowly; after a few stitches you can let go of the loose threads and cut them off.
- keep the machine running smoothly and evenly, and continuously move the fabric underneath the needle; the length of the stitch is determined by how quickly or slowly you move the hoop – aim for small stitches that are close together to create flowing lines.
- keep your movements smooth and build up speed gradually – jerky and sudden changes of direction, speed and tension can break threads and needles.
- because there is no feed dog to grip your fabric you can move the hoop in any direction, enabling you to 'draw' fluid and detailed lines and designs.
- going over your stitched lines twice will give your designs greater definition.

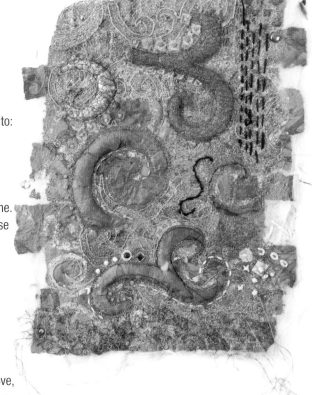

Above: **Wrought sample** (Rachel Lombard). Experimental padding techniques on painted and pieced brown paper. Machine and hand stitch. Below: Holding the hoop and securing the threads for free machine embroidery (Julia Triston).

Using hand and machine stitch creatively

Hand stitching and free machine embroidery can be used separately or combined to create stunning textile surfaces. Once you have gained confidence through your initial explorations, consider some more creative ideas, such as the following:

- go beyond calico to explore other fabric surfaces for free machine embroidery; denim has a different surface quality from silk, as does felt from muslin – experiment.
- if your 'fabric' is substantial and firm enough (for example, thick paper or pelmet Vilene [Pellon]), you don't have to use a hoop.
- paper is a great surface for hand and machine stitch – design work can be stitched into directly, creating mixed-media 'drawings' (if your paper is quite thin, it can be strengthened by fusing it to a fabric backing with Bondaweb [Wonder Under]).
- needles create holes, and piercing is a form of mark-making itself – try running papers or fine metal shims through an unthreaded machine to make flowing, dotted lines and patterns.
- stitched surfaces can be distressed with brushes or sandpaper to raise the fibres and threads, creating a more three-dimensional surface and often producing a softer or aged look.
- your own 'fabrics' can be constructed by machine stitching small pieces of materials, threads, papers, etc. on to a background fabric to create a richly textured surface.
- background fabrics and papers can be cut to any shape or size; try stitching on to long, thin strips of fabric, or squares of paper, rather than rectangles – you don't need to be confined by pre-determined boundaries of commercial sizing.
- edges don't have to be straight or square, or at right angles to each other – they can also be irregular, undulating, ragged, frayed or angular.
- combine different types of surfaces – for example, fabrics and coloured and printed papers can be used together in the same piece.
- layered surfaces can be stitched and then areas cut away to reveal different colours and textures underneath – you can cut away from both the front and the back of your work.
- solid and heavy machine stitching can distort fabrics – this can be exploited and used to create form and three-dimensional surfaces.
- the creative process doesn't have to end with stitch – surfaces can be worked and reworked with print, stitch and embellishments to build rich and individual textiles.

Right: **Book of Brilliant Things Sketchbook** (Rachel Lombard). Machine and hand stitched papers and fabrics.

Above and far left: **Book of Brilliant Things Sketchbook** (Julia Triston). Free machined stitch doodles and words with hand embroidery, buttons and mirrors on decorated and bonded papers and fabrics.

Fabric manipulation

The flexibility and softness of fabric enable it to be manipulated in many different ways to create raised, textured, rippled and lumpy surfaces that can be both regular and irregular. Manipulated surfaces can be used as an embellishment – for example, a ruffle – or as a finished piece, such as a quilted panel. Well-known fabric manipulation techniques include smocking, weaving and shibori, and there are many other ways to manipulate fabric creatively. Here are some ideas:

- tearing: strips of fabric can be torn into different widths, which can then be twisted, plaited, woven, bunched, coiled, gathered or rolled and used as embellishments, edges, decorative additions or joined together to create a new, textured surface.
- scrunching: some natural fabrics, such as calico or linen, can be wetted, screwed up and ironed to press and set creases deliberately into the surface.
- pleating: fabric can be folded into regular and irregular pleats; on a small scale these can be used as a decorative feature, and on a larger scale they can give shape and volume.
- tucking: tucks are deep or shallow folds that are stitched into the fabric, creating a decorative linear pattern across the surface.
- gathering: a line of running stitch (by hand or machine) can be sewn along the edge or across the surface of the fabric or a strip of fabric – this stitched line can be straight or wavy and, when pulled, will create a ruched or ruffled effect.
- shirring: wind shirring elastic on to your sewing machine bobbin by hand (use sewing thread on the top) then, with a long straight stitch, sew lines or grids across your fabric; this will produce a gathered surface that has the advantage of being stretchy and flexible.
- pulling: individual threads and fibres in loosely woven fabrics can be moved by tight hand stitching (or by using a wide zigzag on the machine) to distort the surface and create regular and irregular eyelets, holes, gaps and spaces.

Right: **Felt circles** (Ali Kent). Hand-dyed felt stitched with free machine embroidery to manipulate the surface into raised areas.

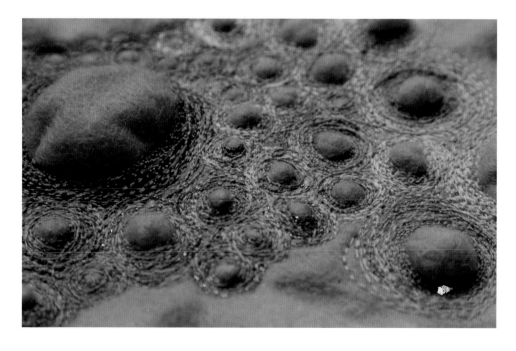

- padding: small areas, or a series of areas, can be raised either by inserting stuffing between layers or by applying padding to the surface underneath a slip.
- shrinking: a textured surface can be made by hand or machine stitching two fabrics together, one of which will shrink when washed at a high temperature and one of which won't, such as calico and a polyester sheer, or wool and a light silk.
- sculpting: fabrics can be soaked in a weak solution of PVA glue and water before being moulded over or inside a three-dimensional item, such as a bowl, or laid over and pushed through a grid – for example, a cooling rack; when dried, they will hold their manipulated form and remain soft enough to stitch into (protect mould with clingfilm [Saran Wrap] first).
- slashing: fabrics can be slit with scissors, sharp blades or a soldering iron to create openings, gashes and holes; these can be made to form regular patterns, and raw edges can be frayed to give extra texture.
- quilting: traditionally, this involves layering two fabrics with a wadding in between, then stitching through all three layers, usually in a regular pattern by hand or machine, to form a layered textile with decorative low relief.

Many of these techniques can be used with papers, plastics and alternative 'fabrics'. Enjoy experimenting and remember to keep a record – as you are going along – of what you are doing, how you did it and what you learned in the process.

Above: **Solar Hanging (detail) 130 x 130cm (51 x 51in)** (Rachel Lombard). Painted and pieced brown paper. Padded and raised areas. Machine and hand stitch.

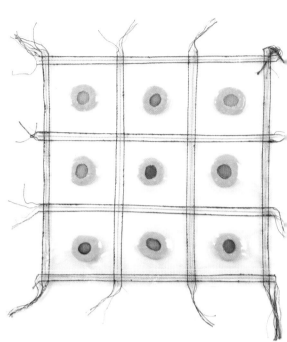

There are many traditional layering and piecing techniques – for example, appliqué, patchwork and quilting. Some contemporary ways of combining and layering 'fabrics', such as trapping and repiecing, and layering and slashing, are an extension and expansion of these methods. Other newer layering and piecing processes have evolved as new products have become available – for example, fusible webbing such as Bondaweb (Wonder Under) that can be used to bond surfaces, threads and fibres together.

Experimental layering and piecing using a wide range of fabrics will enable you to become familiar with their individual properties, such as their opacity and translucency. The possibilities for mixing and combining colours, textures and densities of 'fabrics' are endless.

Right: **Trapping sample** (Julia Triston). Liquorice Allsorts trapped in plastic shower curtain with machine stitching.
Below: **Trapping sample** (Julia Triston). Snippets of threads and fabrics stuffed into bubble wrap, free machine embroidered.

Trapping

This is a layering technique that uses a sheer or transparent 'fabric' over the top of a background to hold in place something in between. The background 'fabric' can be plain or printed and the top layer can be completely see-through (for example, plastic) or coloured (for example, chiffon or netting). The middle layer can be made up from scraps of fabric and threads, beads and sequins, natural and found objects, papers and plastics, powders and glitters, coins and washers, etc. Alternatively, both top and bottom layers can be transparent, allowing the middle layer to be encased in 'fabric' and viewed from both sides. Depending on the content of the middle layer, hand or machine stitch should be used to hold the top and bottom layers in place, permanently trapping the contents.

Repiecing

This technique involves stitching, cutting and repiecing fabrics and threads in an orderly or random way to create a new textile surface. The selected fabrics, threads and recycled materials can be diverse in their textures, densities, weaves and patterns, but there needs to be a unity between them in the colour scheme, tone or theme to make a harmonious whole.

Repiecing involves machine stitching strips of fabric along their edges on to a thin background fabric. Lengths of thread can be laid between the strips and stitched over to hold them in place. The machine stitching can be solid or open, straight or decorative, free or patterned. Once stitched, the newly formed surface is cut into several equally sized squares. These are then repieced in a new formation on to a new thin background fabric and restitched by hand or machine. This process is repeated several times until the original blocks and strips have been broken up, repieced and integrated to form a new textile surface. Bondaweb (Wonder Under) can be used to fuse the blocks and strips to the background before stitching (see page 87) – this will give a less textured result.

Right: Two approaches to repiecing; top (Rachel Lombard) with Bondaweb (Wonder Under), bottom (Julia Triston) without.

Layering and slashing

This technique uses several layers of woven fabric that are stacked on top of each other and stitched by machine in regularly spaced lines along the bias. All but the bottom layer of fabric are then cut through, using very sharp small scissors or a stitch ripper. The raw, cut edges are brushed, either with a suede brush or toothbrush, to raise the fibres and create a 'faux chenille' effect.

The stack can be made from the same type of fabric or a variety of different ones. As this technique relies on creating texture by breaking down and exposing the weave of the fabric, you will discover that some fabrics are more suitable than others – calico, scrim and dupion silk work well, whereas felt, netting and velvet do not.

Left: **Pincushion** (Judith Johnson). Layering and slashing technique on silks, to create a textured surface.

Bonding

This versatile technique is a way of constructing your own small or large-scale backgrounds and 'fabrics', which can be thin, light and lacy, or thick, heavy and dense. Layers of fabrics or snippets are permanently sandwiched together, using Bondaweb (Wonder Under) and/or bonding powder, rather than stitch. Designs can be built up in a random, organized or pictorial way.

Bondaweb (Wonder Under) is a sheet of fusible webbing that acts as a dry 'fabric glue' on a silicone paper backing that can be bought in packs or by the metre. It can be peeled off its backing paper and either used as a sheet on top of, between or underneath fabric layers, or torn into pieces and mixed with the 'fabrics' and snippets, before being ironed. The heat and pressure of the iron will melt the Bondaweb and fuse the layers together.

This technique is a great way of using up fragments of fabrics, thread scraps and recycled materials. Most common, specialist and alternative 'fabrics' and threads can be bonded, although some may melt when heat is applied. By experimenting, you will discover what works best. It is imperative that you always use a top and bottom layer of baking parchment to protect your iron and ironing board when using Bondaweb. The parchment paper will stick to your bonded layers, but can easily be peeled off when cool.

There are many exciting possibilities to explore with this technique. The table below includes some suggestions for ordering your layered materials. Some examples of these techniques are shown overleaf.

BOTTOM LAYER	MIDDLE LAYER 1	MIDDLE LAYER 2	TOP LAYER
solid fabric	Bondaweb (Wonder Under)	snippets	transparent fabric
solid fabric	Bondaweb (Wonder Under)	snippets	Bondaweb (Wonder Under)
transparent fabric	Bondaweb (Wonder Under)	snippets	transparent fabric
Bondaweb (Wonder Under)	snippets	n/a	Bondaweb (Wonder Under)

Chiffons, netting, voiles and organzas are all suitable transparent fabrics for this technique. Suitable solid 'fabrics' include cottons, polycottons, silks, papers and tissue papers. Snippets can be cut, torn or left whole, but need to be quite small. They can be any combination of the following:

- wax crayon shavings
- seeds, leaves and petals
- herbs and spices
- feathers
- glitter
- small beads and sequins
- pencil shavings
- scraps of fabrics, threads and recycled materials
- scraps of papers and tissue papers
- lace
- ribbons and braids
- sweet wrappers and foils
- tinsel
- packaging
- sand

This page: **Bonded samples** (Julia Triston). Experimenting with Bondaweb (Wonder Under) to create fused, layered backgrounds for stitch. Opposite page: **Bonded sandwich** (Julia Triston). Multicoloured and textured snippets sandwiched between two layers of Bondaweb, cut to shape.

Appliqué

Appliqué is the art of decorating one fabric with another. It involves a smaller piece of fabric, or a motif, being applied to a larger background fabric, traditionally with stitch. There are many styles of appliqué throughout the world – for example, the folk appliqué of India, mola work from the San Blas Islands, broderie perse from the UK and arpilleras from Peru. Many of these methods of appliqué rely on bold, contrasting colours to create rich, vibrant and decorative surfaces. Traditional appliqué designs, usually worked in cottons, are stylized and often geometric or symmetrical, as simple shapes are easier to stitch by hand than complex ones. The bonding and machine techniques used in contemporary appliqué enable more complex designs to be worked with a wider variety of fabrics and materials.

Above: **Jain wallhanging from India** (Julia Triston). Detail of layered appliqué surface in cotton and silks.

For each of the following methods it is important to line up the grain of the applied fabric with that of the background fabric. Choose appropriate fabrics and contrasting colours that will suit your design and its purpose. For example, if you are making an appliqué panel for a bag, you will need to work with fabrics that can stand a lot of wear and tear, whereas if you are constructing a delicate wall hanging, you may choose to work with fabrics that are finer or fragile.

Hand appliqué

The best fabrics to use for hand appliqué are like with like – for example, cotton with cotton or felt with felt – as they have the same properties as each other and will wash, wear and drape in the same way. Fabrics that are 100 per cent cotton are often favoured, as the edges of an applied motif can be turned under and creased to produce a crisp edge. As felt is a non-woven fabric without a grain, it has the advantage of not fraying when cut and its edges do not need to be turned under, so more complex motifs can be developed.

When applying your motif to the background fabric, use a sewing thread of the same colour as the motif. Slip stitch it into place with tiny stitches, bringing the needle up through the motif and down into the background fabric, so that the stitches become as 'invisible' as possible. Alternatively, you can create a more decoratively stitched outline, as in crazy patchwork, by using linear hand stitches (for example, buttonhole or feather stitch) with hand embroidery threads.

Above: **Broderie Perse Quilt (detail)** (Mandy Pattullo). Hand appliqué on to a background of recycled, patched fabrics.

Machine appliqué

Machine appliqué is often used on items of clothing and household linen that are frequently washed, such as T-shirts and pillowcases, as it is a more robust method than hand appliqué. This technique gives a strong, visible, 'hard-edged' outline to your applied motif, which becomes an integral part of the design.

In this technique motifs are laid on to a background fabric and secured in place with a line of machine satin stitch (a wide zigzag stitch with a very short length). As the solid line of satin stitch completely covers the raw edge of the motif being applied, there is no need to turn under the edges. Some decorative machine satin stitches can also be used instead of the plainer zigzag.

Turning corners neatly with satin stitch will take practice, as you do not want to end up with lots of overlapping stitches, which could look 'lumpy'. When applying a motif that has an acute angle it is best to reduce the width of the satin stitch gradually as you get nearer to its point.

Motifs can also be applied to a background fabric with free machine embroidery, which leaves a raw, 'softer-edged' finish.

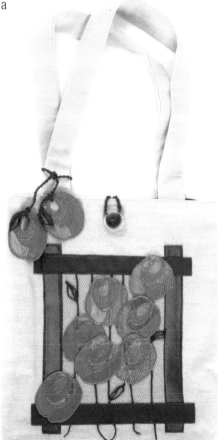

Cut-away appliqué

This is a free machine embroidery technique, also referred to as reverse appliqué, that allows the possibility of a greater exploration of colour, texture and design than the two previous methods.

In this technique layers of fabric are stacked up to form a pile that is stitched through using free machine straight stitch. Selected areas are then cut away close to the stitched boundaries to reveal the fabrics beneath, giving a soft-edged finish.

It is important to go over your stitch lines two or three times to define, and completely outline, your shapes, and to use small, sharp scissors to cut away the layers of fabric. Also, keep your stitches small and close together to prevent excessive fraying when the fabric layers are cut away.

Once this technique is mastered, complex compositions can be quickly developed by:

- cutting away a single layer
- cutting through all the layers to make holes and spaces
- slitting layers and stitching them back
- cutting away layers from both sides to reveal a single middle layer of fabric

This versatile technique gives you the opportunity to create small or large, angular or fluid shapes, patterns and designs. Contrasting weights, colours and textures of fabrics and threads can be combined, allowing you the freedom to experiment and explore without the constraints of tradition.

Left: **Machine appliqué sample** (Yana Krizka). Random layers of fabric applied to background with free machine embroidery. Above right: **Brown Paper sample** (Rachel Lombard) Block-printed, colour-washed brown paper sample, showing cut-away appliqué. See page 42 for the finished piece. Right: **Rose Bag** (Jill Young). Bag with panel of bonded appliquéd roses and border, showing 'hard-edged' outlines.

Bonded appliqué

Bonded appliqué uses Bondaweb (Wonder Under), with the heat of an iron, to fuse one piece of fabric permanently to another. This technique is often used when fine or soft, loosely woven fabrics (for example, muslin, scrim or chiffon) need to be strengthened before they are cut into shapes and applied to another surface. The layer of Bondaweb between the fabrics will not only strengthen and stabilize them but also prevent the cut fabric motif fraying; there is no need to turn under the edges before applying the motif to the background fabric. Once backed with Bondaweb the fabrics become firmer, allowing complex and intricate shapes to be cut out. Depending on the purpose and function of your item, the edges of an applied motif can be left raw or decoratively stitched around with hand or machine embroidery.

Almost any fabric can be bonded to almost any surface – the only limitation is that the iron must be hot enough to melt the Bondaweb without melting the fabrics. However, this could be used to your advantage, as a distressed or melted surface on your fabric may be exactly what you want!

Bonded appliqué needs to be worked in a set order – be careful to keep fabric grains aligned throughout:

- iron the Bondaweb on to the back of the fabric from which the motif will be cut – keep its backing paper in place and remember to use baking parchment paper to protect your iron and ironing board.
- on the backing paper, draw out your motif in reverse and then carefully cut it out.
- peel off the backing paper and lay your motif – Bondaweb side down – on to your background fabric; align the grains if necessary.
- cover with baking parchment and iron to melt the Bondaweb and permanently fix the motif in place.

Discover, part of the Traveller Collection (Rachel Lombard). Printed silk, abaca tissue, machine and hand stitch.

Edges

Every textile piece you make, whether a sample or a finished project, will have edges. It is important to consider how to finish off your pieces from the outset, so that your edges are integral to your overall designs and not just an afterthought. Edges are not necessarily always just at the border or boundary of your stitching; they can be an interruption or a definition within the piece itself – for example, a pin tuck, a line denoting a colour change or a raised cord running across the surface.

An edge can be a decorative feature itself, such as lace around the edge of a tablecloth, or it can be almost unnoticed, where the focus is on the surface of the textile, rather than its boundaries. An edge can be rough or smooth, hard or soft, straight or undulating, looped or knotted, deep or shallow, sculpted or plain, and regular or irregular. It can be embellished on one, two or all sides of your work as appropriate, whereas a border will usually run around the whole piece.

The table below gives you some ideas that you can experiment with to create edges and borders that are either plain and simple or highly decorative.

TYPES OF 'FABRIC' EDGES	TYPES OF STITCHED EDGES	THINGS THAT CAN BE APPLIED TO EDGES
cut	hemmed	fringes
torn	piped	beads and buttons
burnt and melted	bound	prairie points
snipped	machine satin stitched	cords and braids
ruffled	wired	lace and ribbons
frayed	blanket stitched	slips and tabs
knotted	decoratively hand stitched	tassels
raw	free machine embroidered	shisha mirrors
bonded and glued	patterned and scalloped	feathers
embossed	worked on dissolvable fabrics	stretched springs

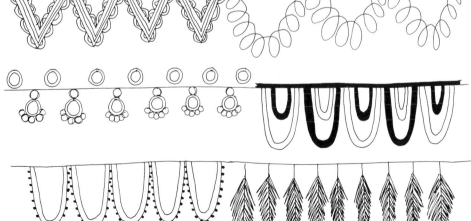

Left: **Experimental edges** (see caption on page 4).

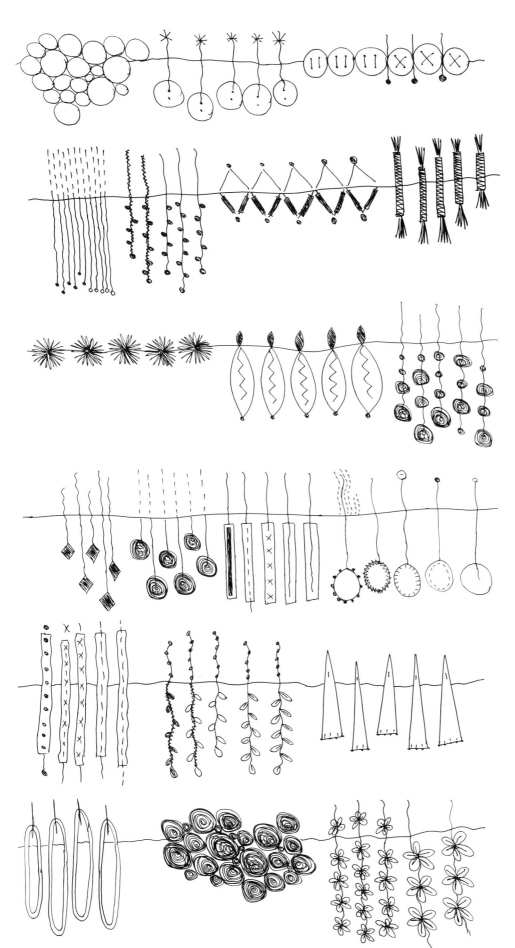

Left: Ideas for edges: overhanging, multiple, repeated, dangling, integrated into the fabric edge (Rachel Lombard). Opposite page, bottom right: Drawings for edges showing ideas for using lace, stretched springs, eyelets, bells, rouleaux and feathers (Julia Triston).

Embellishments

An embellishment will add a focus, a highlight, a sparkle or a decorative detail to a surface. It can be a single motif or part of a repeating pattern. Many traditional and unconventional items can be used to embellish and enhance a surface, as shown in the table below. Many everyday, or throwaway, items can make great embellishments for your textiles. Be creative and inventive – experiment with the unusual and unexpected – but stay focused and keep your embellishments appropriate to your sources of inspiration and your design development work.

HABERDASHERY	RECYCLED MATERIALS	NATURAL ITEMS	DIY MATERIALS	METALS	HANDMADE ITEMS
sequins	bottle tops	feathers	washers	tomato purée	rolled paper beads
beads	toothpaste tube	quills	tile spacers	tubes	moulded glue
mirrors	tops	beetle wings	wires	drink cans	dissolvable fabric
buttons and	packaging	shells	fuses	ring pulls	motifs
toggles	sweetie wrappers	bones	garden mesh	broken	machine-wrapped
fringing	foils	hair	rope and twine	jewellery	cords
frogging and	cocktail sticks	pebbles	cup hooks	brads	stuffed cords
rouleaux	inner tubing	stones and	picture hooks	paperclips	knotted ribbons
zips	Christmas	gems	cable clips and ties	staples	slips
braids and cords	decorations	seeds	chains	hair clips	'clay' buttons,
tassels	plastics	driftwood	plastic tubing	keys	toggles and beads
lace	carrier bags	sea glass	hinges	badges	pompoms
ribbons	bus tickets	grasses	nuts and bolts	fishing weights	tassels
press studs	stamps	leaves	plant labels	curtain rings	twisted cords
hooks and eyes	shoelaces	canes	nails and	jewellery	ruffles and frills
eyelets	elastic bands	twigs and	screws	findings	crocheted edges
suspender clips	corks	bark	springs	shims	felted balls

Conclusion to Part 3

Above: **Embellished sample** (Janice MacDougall). Buttons and beads on pins, on a stitched and heat-distressed background.

The creative process of experimenting with materials and sampling is about progressing your ideas from your source materials through design and into stitch, while remaining true to your original ideas and intentions, and being flexible enough to be open to making new discoveries along the way. Not all of your experiments will be successful, and you will eliminate techniques and materials that you don't like, but through trying, testing and learning, your work will become richer, more expressive and increasingly individual.

In Part 4 we will look at finalizing your designs, creating your resolved textile piece, and evaluating the processes and outcomes.

Above left: **Medieval Tile** (Kathleen Thompson). Symmetrical composition stitched by hand with embellishments of hooks, eyes, press studs and beads. Above: **Handmade Tassel** (Janice MacDougall). Hand embroidery and beading on handmade felt. Far left: **Nine Covered Buttons** (Rachel Lombard). Machine and hand stitch on silk. Left: **Face Brooch** (Karine Richardson). Hand embroidery on cotton.

PART 4 : MAKING AND EVALUATING

Chapter 6

FINALIZING DESIGNS AND CREATING YOUR OWN TEXTILE

Left: **Book of Brilliant Things** (Julia Triston). Detail of finger painting highlighted with coloured pencils, embellished with hand stitch and buttons.

This chapter is all about bringing together the ideas and processes that you have explored in previous chapters. It will also encourage you to review and critically evaluate your work, the progress you have made, and the direction your creative journey may take.

Taking stock

At this stage of the creative process it is important to take stock of where you are. Reviewing your original plans and mind maps, and reconnecting with your source materials, is a valuable step towards finalizing ideas for your resolved textile piece. Looking back through and reflecting on the stages of gathering, exploring, developing, sampling and experimenting will remind you of where you started and what inspired your personal journey.

There will come a point when it is time to move on from sampling. Maybe this is because you have run out of ideas, have a looming deadline and must move on, want to develop one of your samples in more depth, or have reached a natural conclusion.

Take a good look back through your design work and samples. What common themes emerge from your body of work? Is there a particular design element that dominates, or a shape, pattern, colour, technique or material that you want to continue working with? You might be surprised by the direction your work has taken, and be looking forward to taking your design into the making stage.

What are you going to make?

Before making your final decision about how to make your textile, you will have many choices to consider about what to make. One of the initial considerations is whether your item is going to be two-dimensional or three-dimensional. The table opposite gives some ideas.

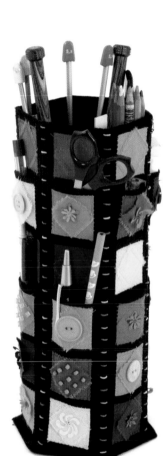

Above: **The Tower** (Vicky Hutchinson). Pencil pot: Hand-embroidered hexagonal construction from mountboard, felt, appliquéd fabric and paper.

Right: **Panel in box lid** (Rachel Lombard). Hand-dyed muslins layered and slashed with machine and hand stitch.

Above: **Deeds not Words pincushion** (Julia Triston). Machine appliqué on silk, with handmade tassels, stuffed with sawdust.

IDEAS FOR TWO-DIMENSIONAL ITEMS

panels (part of a cushion, bag, book
   cover, box, hat or garment)
wall hangings
belts
table runners and tablecloths
aprons
curtains
blinds
coasters
quilts
scarves
pictures
chess or game boards
fire screens
seat covers
banners
samplers

IDEAS FOR THREE-DIMENSIONAL ITEMS

cushions
jewellery
boxes
bags
hats, shoes and gloves
chatelaines
masks
ruffs, cuffs and collars
books
bowls
mobiles and decorations
soft toys and dolls
pincushions and needle cases
pencil cases and make-up bags
installations
egg and tea cosies
clocks

Below left: **Alice in Wonderland Unbirthday Cake** (Ailish Henderson). Manipulated fabric on felt, card and wire base with handmade embellishments. Height 55cm (21½in). Below: **An Eye for an Eye panel** (Julia Triston). Free machined text and drawing on painted fabric with hand stitch and buttons.

Two-dimensional items often focus more on surface decoration, whereas three-dimensional items place more emphasis on construction. Both can be decorative and functional.

Writing a brief

Setting yourself a brief with targets to achieve in your completed piece will help to clarify what you are working towards. Quite often you may have constraints to take into consideration when planning and making your finished pieces. These will determine the boundaries that you work within and can allow you to make positive choices about how your work will progress.

Here are a few questions to ask yourself before writing a brief for your project:

What research do you need to do before making your final decisions? It is important to see what others have done, to set your work within its proper context.
- does your item need to fit in with a particular style, setting or colour theme?
- does your item need to include a specific mechanism – for example, to fasten or hang?
- how have other artists or makers responded to a similar theme or similar constraints?

Do you have a specific budget? Remember that everything costs – including your own time.
- do you have a limit to what you can spend on materials?
- have you been given a commission with a budget?
- are there presentation costs to consider – for example, for framing or mounting?
- do you have transport or postage expenses to consider – for example, Special Delivery or courier costs for an exhibition?

Do you have a deadline? Be realistic about what you can achieve in the time you have.
- are you working towards an exhibition or competition entry date?
- do you need to deliver your work for a specific event or occasion?
- are you working on a commission that has a completion date?

Are there 'site specific' considerations? It is important to take these issues into account at this planning stage.
- what light sources will your work be exposed to – do you need to work with light-fast fabrics?
- will your item need to be washed frequently – for example, a child's quilt?
- does your work need to be protected behind glass – for example, in a dusty environment or a busy thoroughfare?
- once your item is complete, what other issues will you need to take into consideration? For example, in all situations it is important to label your work and packaging clearly – you may not always be the next person to unpack or repack your work.
- if you are making a piece of work for an exhibition, you will need to consider packaging and transportation.
- if you are making three-dimensional pieces, storage will need to be carefully addressed.
- if you are storing textiles for any length of time, you will have to wrap them in acid-free tissue paper and protect them from damp, light and insects.

Consider from the outset what is going to happen to your work when you have completed it, and how it is going to be used and viewed. Some textiles will be loved and well used, and will therefore have a limited life span. Your stitched textiles should be enjoyed, celebrated and used for their purpose.

Making and using patterns and maquettes

When thinking about how to make your item, dimensions must be taken into account. For two-dimensional pieces you will need to consider heights, lengths and widths. You may have to use patterns and templates to work out the balance and proportions of your designs. For three-dimensional items you will also need to consider the depth and form of your piece. As well as using patterns and templates, it may be necessary to make a maquette in order to work out the practicalities of construction.

Commercial patterns

These are widely available through magazines, shops and online outlets, and are often bought for garments, bags, soft toys and furnishings. Commercial patterns are useful because:

- they can teach you a lot about construction methods and techniques.
- they give clear assembly instructions.
- they provide a tried and tested structure and framework to work within.
- someone else has done the working out for you, so they can save you a lot of time.
- they can sometimes be adapted to fit your own ideas.

However, relying on commercial patterns can be limiting, expensive, sometimes complicated, and may lead you to make compromises within your work.

Below: **Egypt Sketchbook** (Julia Triston). Drawing and carbon-paper tracing template for collar on The Return of the Lost Soul (detail shown on page 106).

Making your own templates and patterns

It can be exciting to make your own templates and patterns. These can emerge directly from the shapes and patterns of your source materials and design work. It can be a time-consuming process, but is rewarding because:

- it enables you to produce finished work that is directly relevant to and reflective of your source materials.
- it is more likely to lead to a unique and individual product.
- it is an exciting and innovative way to express your ideas and further develop your design skills.

Below: **Paper pattern pieces for Brown Paper Bag** (Rachel Lombard). Pieces for the bag's body and handle, also showing design development. The bag is shown on page 42.

When making your own templates and patterns, use robust materials (for example, lining paper or pattern paper) that will stand up to constant use and handling. It is essential to label all individual template and pattern pieces clearly, and to keep detailed records of the order of work and assembly instructions – don't assume that you will remember the next time round, because we know from experience you won't.

Making maquettes

Making a maquette gives you the opportunity to examine scale and proportion physically and see exactly how your item will function. Producing a maquette from cheap fabrics and materials, such as calico, pelmet Vilene (Pellon), cardboard, glue and tape, will save you time in the long run because it gives you the chance to change and resolve any construction issues before starting to work with your precious materials.

Maquettes can be made to test out a whole design (for example, a box and its lid or a bag and its lining), or just a part or aspect of it, such as:

- hinges
- clips
- straps
- joins
- seam allowances
- handles
- folds
- fastenings
- borders
- edges
- hanging mechanisms
- weight
- balance
- stability
- proportions

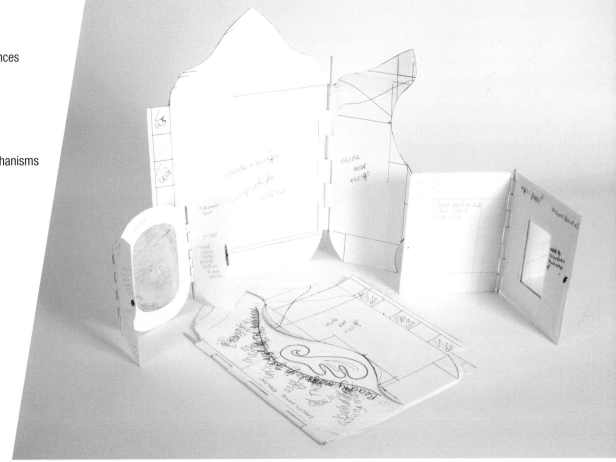

Maquettes can be made to scale or actual size. A word of warning – make sure that your maquettes take into account the properties of your chosen final materials – for instance, a sample box made in calico will be thinner than the same box made in quilted fabrics and, as a consequence, the lid dimensions will need to be adjusted.

Above: **Maquettes for Mermaid Mirror** (Rachel Lombard). Trying out shapes, hinges and construction ideas. The finished piece is shown on page 119.

Order of work

After finalizing your designs and deciding how you are going to achieve them, it is worth making a comprehensive, step-by-step list that sets out each stage of your working process. This will help you to work in a logical and consistent way, limit your mistakes and save time. It also provides you with a list against which to check your progress.

Keeping notes and making adjustments

Below: **The Return of the Lost Soul** (detail) (Julia Triston). Free machine embroidery on abaca tissue, organzas, felt and dissolvable fabrics on a handmade paper background with applied human hair.

Keeping notes as you go along – in your sketchbook or on your templates, pattern pieces and maquettes – will enable you to remember your order of work and any adjustments you made in the making process. Recording any changes will save you time if you make that item again. Making adjustments is about learning as you work and being open to your design evolving and changing. This may mean reassessing your choice of materials or techniques, or simplifying your designs as your work progresses. Just changing seam allowances or repositioning buttons can really make a difference and strengthen the balance of your overall design. Remember that successful outcomes don't always have to follow a linear process.

Recording time taken

It is useful to get into the habit of recording how long it takes you to make an item, as time costs. This is good working practice if you are planning to sell your work, or put a value on it for insurance purposes.

Knowing when to stop

How do you know when your item is complete? This is sometimes a difficult decision to make. To help you to decide, ask yourself the following questions:

- does your finished article function as you designed it to?
- does your item look complete?
- is your textile piece visually pleasing?
- does your end result reflect your aims, message, source materials and ideas?

If your answer to all of these questions is 'yes' – well done! It is now time to stop. If, however, you cannot answer 'yes' to all of the above questions, it is a good idea to:

- ask for feedback from others – get their honest opinions and reflect on their suggestions.
- leave your item *in situ* – this will give you the opportunity to look at it from all angles and view it at different times of the day.
- put it away for a few days – sometimes you can get too familiar with your work and need distance to really see what is in front of you; a psychological break from it can do you good.
- consider if you are becoming obsessed with tiny surface details – these may be important to you now, but others will be viewing your work as a whole, and won't be as aware of the minutiae as you are.
- think about what isn't working – this could be something as simple as your choice of clasps, length of handles, size of tassels or style of edging – things that may be easy to rectify.

This is the process we use for moving our work forwards until we are satisfied that our finished pieces meet our expectations. Even if you would make your item in a slightly different way next time, it is important to be happy with the outcome and proud of your final piece. In time you will discover what works and what doesn't, and you will gain the confidence to make a positive choice about when to stop and when to carry on.

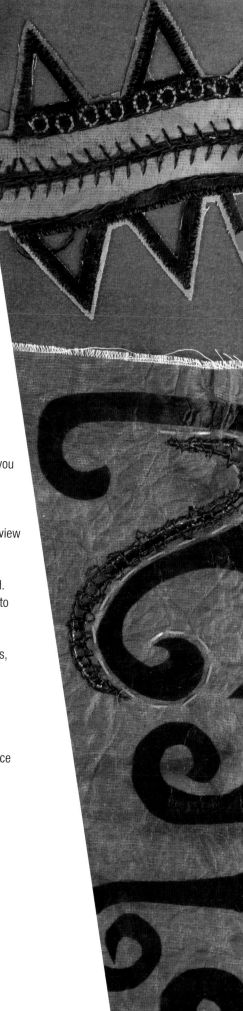

Right: **Detail of
Beauty Sketchbook page**
(Rachel Lombard).

Presentation

Some textile pieces will need to be formally presented to show them off at their best or to protect their delicate surfaces. An embroidered panel may need to be framed after lacing (that is, stretched over strong card and felt padding, then stitched across the back to hold it firmly in place), or a sampler may need to be mounted behind glass. The choices for mounting and presenting your work are numerous and can range widely in price.

Textiles can be presented directly upon mountboard, which is relatively cheap and can be cut to any size. Alternatively, a textile can be displayed behind a window cut from mountboard. Boards come in many colours and textures; sometimes you may choose to double-mount your work.

Work can be solely mounted using board or it can be framed as well. You will have to consider what impact the style of frame will have on your work – it could either enhance it or overwhelm it. Heavily textured textiles will need to be set into deeper frames, especially if you intend to glaze them. Frames can be custom-made to your individual specifications by professionals, or bought ready-made in a range of standard sizes.

Textiles behind glass can often appear flat and lifeless, as much of the surface texture will be less apparent, but in some cases it is important to protect work in a glazed frame – glass can be plain, tinted or non-reflective. As a creative alternative to glass, textiles can be encased between, or hung behind, sheets of Perspex. Other items may not need to be framed, but may still need protecting behind glass – for example, in a display cabinet.

Environmental factors, such as dust, light, temperature and humidity, can affect the way you present your work and should be taken into account from the outset. All aspects of presentation need to be very carefully considered, as they can greatly enhance your work or completely detract from it. Your chosen style of presentation must suit the purpose, function and design of your textile, enabling it to speak for itself.

Below: **Crewel Work Sampler** (Tracy A Franklin). Shows hand stitching on front (left) and lacing on back (right).

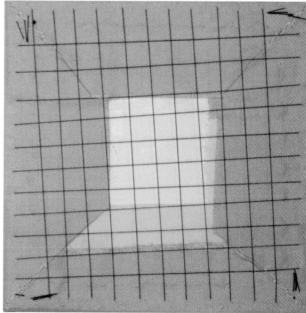

Left: **Getting Ready to Go Out!, part of the Beauty Collection** (Rachel Lombard). Glossy magazine paper, printed silk slips, machine-wrapped cord. Machine and hand stitch. 19 x 19cm (7½ x 7½in). Bottom left: **Factory Floor** (Rachel Lombard). Compressed silk loops with hand stitch into mount, framed behind glass. Below right: **Lace Fragment** (Julia Triston). Stitched paper panel secured onto layered, frayed fabric, framed behind glass.

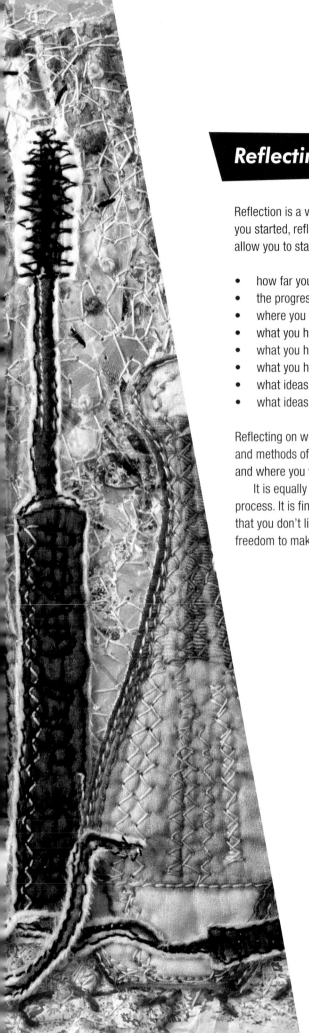

Reflecting on your progress

Reflection is a vital part of the creative process. It is valuable to take the time to look back at where you started, reflect upon the journey you have made, and take stock of where you are now. This will allow you to start thinking about:

- how far you have come
- the progress you have made
- where you want to go next
- what you have learned in the process
- what you have enjoyed
- what you have not enjoyed
- what ideas you have chosen and developed
- what ideas you rejected and left behind

Reflecting on what you have liked and enjoyed, such as discovering new materials, product ranges and methods of working, is rewarding and inspiring because it reaffirms and clarifies where you are and where you want to go next.

It is equally useful to reflect on what you have disliked or discarded during this creative process. It is fine to give yourself permission to leave behind methods, materials and techniques that you don't like, or found too complicated, irrelevant or time-consuming. This will give you the freedom to make positive choices about your future work.

Left: **Getting Ready to Go Out!** (detail) (Rachel Lombard).

Evaluation

When you have completed your textile project it is always a good idea to formally evaluate your working process and the finished item as objectively as possible. The following list of questions will give you a framework to use at the conclusion of each body of work:

What have I learned?
- what learning was useful and why?
- what skills have I revisited and how have I used them?
- have I discovered new skills, materials, products, suppliers, tools and equipment?
- why did I choose one technique, material or product over another?

What would I do differently?
- would I change my order of work?
- could I simplify the processes that I used and, if so, how?
- could I have worked in different colourways?
- could I have worked on a different scale?
- should I have chosen different materials?
- what are the advantages and disadvantages of the materials and methods I chose to use?
- what alternative methods of presentation could I have used?

Do I want to continue to develop this theme or idea?
- if so, why and how?
- if not, why not?
- could I develop a series of related items – for example, a pincushion, needle case and chatelaine?
- could I produce my work to sell commercially?
- could I develop a different element of my design work or source material?

We strongly recommend that you take time to write down your evaluation, which should be an honest and realistic account of your progress. Looking back at your evaluation will remind you of where you were at that particular point in your creative journey and how your decisions shaped the development of your work, and inform your future textile art.

Right: **Coloured print sample** (Ruth Issett). Ruth is known for her strong use of colour. In this sample she used Markal Paintstiks and fabric printing colour on a calico background.

Conclusion

Throughout this book we have aimed to give you the confidence and tools to demystify the process of creating your own stitched textiles from your own designs.

How to be Creative in Textile Art can be used as a guide, a reference book, or an instruction manual and resource that can be dipped in and out of, or used when your creativity needs a boost. While we are offering a progressive and logical step-by-step approach, ultimately there is no right and wrong way of working. In time you will develop your own working practice, and adapt methods, techniques and materials to suit your textile art projects and to reflect your individuality.

Our aim has been to open your eyes to the endless possibilities and opportunities that can be discovered when gathering raw materials, selecting a theme, setting boundaries, and learning to examine the familiar in detail. We want to encourage you to connect confidently with your innate creativity, to be inspired, and to have the freedom to enjoy making the choices that you know are right for your work.

Your skills, confidence and judgement will continue to grow as you become more experienced and accomplished in your working practice. It is important to keep reviewing and evaluating where you are, and to ask yourself 'why?' when reflecting on your work as a whole. Questioning yourself is an integral part of the working process and will help to move you forwards, enabling you to develop a more expressive and richer body of work.

Every creative journey generates unique challenges and opportunities for innovation, expression and progression. What you learn from every one of your journeys will enrich and enhance your future textile pieces.

We both have a passion for textiles and stitch, and have our own very distinct and individual styles of working. We are enthusiastic about learning through our professional practice, and we are constantly striving to develop original, thought-provoking and innovative textile art works. We enjoy sharing and passing on our skills, through designing, making, exhibiting, selling, teaching and writing. The processes we have laid out in this book are our tried and tested framework for making successfully resolved and rewarding art textiles. We hope our book will excite, inspire and encourage you to give it a go and say, 'I want to do that and I'm not afraid to try!'

Julia Triston
Octopus Hat
20 x 7cm (8 x 2¾in)
Free machine embroidery, raised and padded motifs, hand stitch and beading on painted calico.

Julia Triston
Waking
40 x 40cm (16 x 16in) canvas
Appliqué and cut-away appliqué,
couching, free machine
embroidery and embellishments
on a monoprinted background.

Julia Triston
Toran
142 x 38cm (56 x 15in)
Appliquéd motifs on silks and velvets with hand
and machine embroidery, and embellishments of
shells, mirrors, tomato purée tubes, bells, buttons,
beads, ribbons and sequins.

Rachel Lombard
Elk Box
9 x 16 x 16cm (3½ x 6¼ x 6¼in)
Box made from handmade felt with machine and hand stitch.
The lid is decorated with a grid of woven felt stitched into with
French knots and twisted chain stitches. It is edged with
machine stitch, French knots and running stitch. The words
read 'She held his hand tightly, "What do elk eat Daddy?" '
Inspired by a family holiday in Norway and an unexpected
meeting with an elk.

Rachel Lombard
Lion Box
6 x 15 x 15cm (2½ x 6 x 6in)
Hand-stitched box, hand-dyed cotton and silk with cotton
threads. The lion motif is heavily padded and applied to the lid.
The hill is green silk and the foliage a twisted cord with leaves
and flowers of buttonhole stitch. The words read ' "Will you
always be here?" "Yes I will" said the lion'. Inspired by a much
loved childrens' storybook.

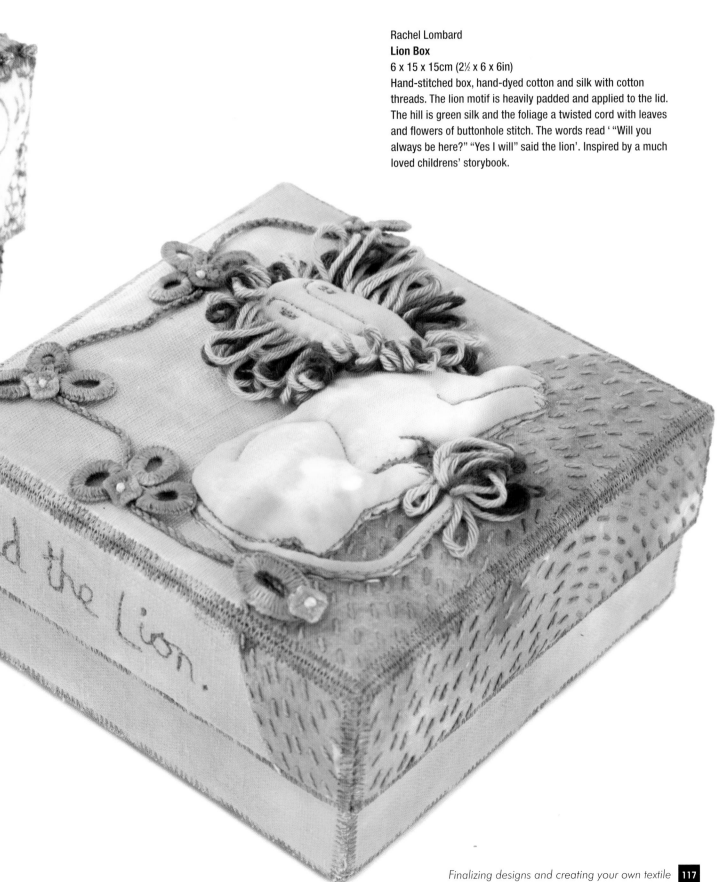

Rachel Lombard
Pink Doc Marten, from the 'I Love Shoes' Collection
10 x 10 cm (4 x 4in)
Glossy magazine paper, printed silk slip, machine and
hand stitch. Shoes take on and reflect the identity of
the wearer.

Rachel Lombard
Mermaid Mirror
40 x 58cm (16 x 23in) when laid flat
Cotton wool paper, twisted chain stitch, applied motifs of
'snip' fabric. Made to illustrate the phrase 'beauty is in the
eye of the beholder, but it's what's inside that counts', which
is machine stitched into the back cover of the mirror.

Julia Triston
Portrait 1
40 x 32cm (16 x 12½in)
Various appliquéd fabrics on cotton,
with hand stitch and free machine
embroidery, and embellishments of
shells, mirrors and buttons.

GENERAL

- Cover all surfaces with plastic sheeting when you are working with art materials.
- Equipment for dyeing should be kept separate from general kitchen equipment to avoid contamination of foodstuffs.
- If you are producing fumes, or working with powders, a face mask should be worn.
- We recommend that you wear gloves and an apron when working with dyes and paints.
- Always follow the manufacturer's instructions when making up dyes or using specialist products.
- It is advisable to wear a face mask and keep your work space well ventilated when using chemicals and heat tools (irons, heat guns, soldering irons, hairdryers), as they can produce fumes.
- Electrical equipment must be kept away from water, switched off when not in use, and serviced regularly.
- Don't leave electrical cables, flexes and wires trailing across floors and work spaces.
- It is important to clear up any spillages immediately.
- Wash all equipment – for example brushes, printing blocks, rollers and printing plates – in warm, soapy water before they dry and harden.

STITCHING

- Keep needles and pins out of the reach of children and pets.
- Dispose of broken needles carefully.
- When free machining we recommend that you use a darning foot, rather than a bare needle; this protects fingers.
- Be careful when machining into metal, as small shards can fly off as the metal starts to fragment.

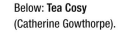

Below: **Tea Cosy**
(Catherine Gowthorpe).

BLEACH

- Bleach is a hazardous chemical and it should always be used with care.
- Ventilate your working area and avoid breathing in fumes – take regular fresh-air breaks.
- Work surfaces should be protected with a plastic sheet.
- Clothing should be protected with an apron.
- Gloves should be worn to avoid contact with the skin.
- Goggles should be worn to protect your eyes.
- Wash all equipment that has been in contact with bleach as quickly as possible after use.
- Do not use sponges or brushes made from natural fibres to apply bleach, as they will disintegrate.

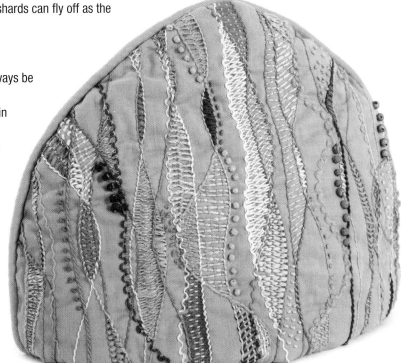

Glossary

abaca tissue
Available in two different weights and can be bought dyed or undyed – it is like a fabric tissue paper, so can be torn easily, but it has a high 'wet strength'.

acute angle
An angle that is less than 90 degrees.

Angelina fibres
Soft and sparkly polyester fibres that can be bonded to make surfaces for textile art.

baking parchment
A silicone-based non-stick paper used to protect your iron and surface – grease-proof paper is not a substitute.

Bondaweb (Wonder Under)
An iron-on fusible webbing with a non-stick paper backing.

bonding powder
A fabric glue in powder form.

Brusho
A non-toxic, dry crystalline powder that is mixed in cold water to form a transparent watercolour.

buckram
A very stiff cotton fabric that can either be sculpted or wetted with cold water and moulded over a form.

chatelaine
A set of short chains attached to a belt worn for carrying keys, scissors, thimbles and other sewing items.

cotton wool paper
A constructed 'textile' surface for stitch made from thin layers of cotton wool fibres bonded with wallpaper paste.

couching
The process of decoratively attaching a thread or object to a surface with stitch.

crazy patchwork
The technique of piecing irregular shapes of recycled and scrap fabrics on to a foundation fabric with bold, decorative stitches to cover the joins.

dissolvable fabrics
Fabrics that can be stitched into before being dissolved, either by heat or with water, so that only the stitching remains.

fabric bias
An imaginary line that cuts across the fabric grain at an angle of 45 degrees – fabric pulled in this direction will stretch and distort.

fabric grain
Woven fabrics are made from threads that run vertically (warp) and horizontally (weft) – when pulled along the warp or weft the fabric remains stable and lacks stretch.

frogging
A decorative fastening, often made from rouleaux or braid.

gutta
An outliner used in silk painting.

jewellery findings
Small metal pieces (fastenings, clips, ear wires, etc.) that are used in jewellery-making.

jute scrim
A natural-fibre material with a very loosely woven mesh.

Khadi papers
Handmade cotton-fibre papers from India.

Lutradur
A non-woven fabric, which comes in different weights – it can be coloured, stitched, heat-distressed or run through an inkjet printer.

machine satin stitch
A stitch used to form a continuous solid line – the machine is set on a wide zigzag setting, with a short stitch length, so that the stitches lie very close together on the fabric.

maquette
A model that is a rough draft, made to work through ideas and issues before embarking on the final piece.

Markal Paintstiks
A brand of oil sticks that are suitable for use on fabric.

Marlitt
A 100% rayon, 4-ply stranded embroidery thread that has a rich lustre. It comes in a wide range of high-sheen colours.

metal threads
A wide range of specialist metal threads that are used in traditional goldwork techniques, such as purls and Japanese gold threads.

motif
A single shape or design that can be repeated to form a pattern.

Nymo
A very strong nylon thread that comes in a variety of colours and is commonly used for beading.

pelmet Vilene (Pellon)
A thick, firm, unwoven interfacing that can be easily cut, shaped and stitched into.

prairie points
Folded triangles of fabric that are used as a decorative

feature within a design, or applied to the edge of a textile, such as a quilt; also known as 'saw tooth edging'.

resolved textile
A piece of work that is complete, finished, fulfils its purpose and meets your expectations.

rolled paper beads
Made by rolling, then securing, a long triangular piece of paper round a fine stick or needle (which is taken out when the bead is formed).

rouleau
A flexible fabric tube – made by cutting and sewing a strip of fabric on the bias, then turning it inside out – used to make ornamental fastenings and frogging.

shibori
A Japanese method of gathering, manipulating and dyeing fabrics.

shirring elastic
A thread-like elastic that can be used on the bottom bobbin of a sewing machine to create a stretchy, gathered surface when stitched.

shisha mirrors
Small pieces of glass (usually round), which are used as an

embellishment, most often in Indian embroidery.

sinamay
A natural-fibre fabric used to create form in millinery.

slip
A small piece of embroidery that is worked first and then applied to a background fabric.

stitch ripper
A small, sharp tool used to help unpick seams or individual stitches, or to slash through fabric layers.

tessellation
Geometric shapes that fit together without leaving any spaces between them.

texture gel
A medium containing specific 'granules' (for example, sand, lava, glass or mica flakes) that can be used alone or mixed with paints to give body and structure to art and design work.

tissue silk
A fabric woven with fine metal and silk threads.

tjanting
A traditional tool used in batik to apply hot wax to fabric.

toran
A decorative and symbolic door hanging from India, adorned with embroidery, mirrors and hanging pendants.

Tyvek
A strong, non-woven material that can be painted and stitched, then distorted with a heat tool.

wireform
A metal mesh that will hold its shape when manipulated; it can easily be moulded over a three-dimensional object, such as a bowl, and can be stitched into.

Xpandaprint
A paint that puffs up when heated with a heat tool.

Opposite page:
Clyde Olliver
Fellside Strip
Length 166cm (65in), width 14cm (5½in) at widest point, depth 2cm (¾in) maximum
Clyde is known for his strong use of line. In this piece materials are shards of slate secured to a slate 'spine' by means of stitches. The slate has to be drilled first to allow the stitches to go right through the work, holding it together. The thread is waxed linen.
Photograph: Lucy Barden.

Further reading

Beaney, Jan and Littlejohn, Jean, *Complete Guide to Creative Embroidery*, Anova Books, 1997

Beaney, Jan and Littlejohn, Jean, *Stitch Magic: Ideas and Interpretation*, Anova Books, 1999

Campbell-Harding, Valerie, *Fabric Painting for Embroidery*, Anova Books, 2001

Creative Publishing, *Textile Art: A Practical and Inspirational Guide to Manipulating, Colouring and Embellishing Fabrics*, Apple Press, 2005

Franklin, Tracy A., *New Ideas in Goldwork*, Anova Books, 2008

Greenlees, Kay, *Creating Sketchbooks for Embroiderers and Textile Artists*, Anova Books, 2005

Holmes, Val, *Creative Recycling in Embroidery*, Anova Books, 2006

Holmes, Val, *Encyclopedia of Machine Embroidery*, Anova Books, 2003

Holmes, Val, *The Machine Embroiderer's Workbook*, Anova Books, 2001

Issett, Ruth, *Colour on Paper and Fabric*, Anova Books, 2000

Thomas, Mary and Eaton, Jan, *Mary Thomas's Dictionary of Embroidery Stitches*, Hodder & Stoughton, 1998

Watts, Pamela, *Beginner's Guide to Machine Embroidery*, Search Press, 2003

Wolff, Colette, *The Art of Manipulating Fabric*, Krause Publications, 1996

Below: **Shatweh Wedding Hat (detail)** (Val Arif). Background constructed from an old woollen scarf, heavily embellished by hand with couching, beads, coins and metal threads.

Organizations

The Batik Guild
www.batikguild.org.uk
The Batik Guild aims to promote and improve education in the art and craft of batik.

The Embroiderers' Guild
Apartment 41
Hampton Court Palace
Surrey
KT8 9AU
Tel: 0208 943 1229
www.embroiderersguild.com
The Embroiderers' Guild works to promote and develop embroidery in the UK through a nationwide network of local guilds. The Guild publishes *Embroidery* and *Stitch* magazines.

The Textile Society
PO Box 1012
St Albans
Hertfordshire
AL1 9NE
Tel: 0207 359 7678
www.textilesociety.org.uk
The Textile Society promotes the study of textile disciplines and celebrates the history and culture of textiles, both traditional and contemporary.

Left: **Rolled beads** (Janice MacDougall). Beads handmade from fabric. Right: **Eyelets** (Ali Kent). Free machine embroidery on patterned fabric with free machined flower and circle made on Pelmet Vilene (Pellon).

Suppliers

Art Van Go
The Studios
1 Stevenage Road
Knebworth
Hertfordshire
SG3 6AN
Tel: 01438 814946
www.artvango.co.uk
Vast range of art and surface decoration supplies, including Brusho, papers, Markal Paintstiks, all-purpose safety masks and wireform

Barnyarns (Ripon) Ltd
Canal Wharf
Bondgate Green
Ripon
North Yorkshire
HG4 1AQ
Tel: 01765 690069
www.barnyarns.co.uk
Wide range of machine embroidery threads, needles and accessories

Bernina Sewing Machines
Tel: 0207 549 7849
www.bernina.co.uk
Information and advice about Bernina products and local stockists

Colourcraft (C&A) Ltd
Unit 6
555 Carlisle Street East
Sheffield
South Yorkshire
S4 8DT
Tel: 0114 242 1431
www.colourcraftltd.com
Manufacturers and distributors of fabric dyes and paints, including Brusho powders

Craftynotions Ltd
Unit 2
Jessop Way
Newark
Nottinghamshire
NG24 2ER
Tel: 01636 700862
www.craftynotions.com
Suppliers of art and surface decoration, materials for creative textile arts

Husqvarna Sewing Machines
Tel: 01527 519480
www.husqvarnaviking.com
Information and advice about Husqvarna products and local stockists

Janome Sewing Machines
Tel: 0161 666 6011
www.janome.co.uk
Information and advice about Janome products and local stockists

Kemtex Educational Supplies
Chorley Business & Technology Centre
Euxton Lane
Chorley
Lancashire
PR7 6TE
Tel: 01257 230220
www.kemtex.co.uk
Suppliers of colour dyes and auxiliaries for dyeing and printing textiles

Oliver Twists
22 Phoenix Road
Crowther
Washington
Tyne & Wear
NE38 0AD
Tel: 0191 416 6016
Email: olivertwistsretail@fsmail.net
Specialist dyers and suppliers of a wide range of hand and machine embroidery threads, fibres, felt and fabrics

Texere Yarns Ltd
College Mill
Barkerend Road
Bradford
West Yorkshire
BD1 4AU
Tel: 01274 722191
www.texere-yarns.co.uk
Wide range of dyed and undyed threads and yarns useful for hand embroidery

Textile Techniques
37 High Street
Bishop's Castle
Shropshire
SY9 5BE
Tel: 01588 638712
www.textiletechniques.co.uk
Batik supplies, tjantings, wax and dyes

The Pink Pig Company
Emley Business Park
Emley
nr Huddersfield
West Yorkshire
HD8 9QY
Tel: 01924 840759
www.the-pink-pig.co.uk
Sketchbooks in a wide range of colours, sizes and shapes

Whaleys (Bradford) Ltd
Harris Court
Great Horton
Bradford
West Yorkshire
BD7 4EQ
Tel: 01274 576718
www.whaleys-bradford.ltd.uk
Enormous range of fabrics and interfacings – many suitable for dyeing – including calico, silks, pelmet Vilene (Pellon), Bondaweb (Wonder Under) and dissolvable fabrics

Julia Triston
Studio 2
Fowlers Yard
Back Silver Street
Durham
DH1 3RA
Tel: 0191 383 0831
www.juliatriston.com
Workshops, dayschools, residencies and courses in contemporary art, design and world textiles

Rachel Lombard
Tel: 07986 852587
www.rachellombardtextileart.talktalk.net
Contemporary stitched textile art and design, workshops and illustrated talks. Based in County Durham

Tracy A Franklin
Studio 3
Fowlers Yard
Back Silver Street
Durham
DH1 3RA
Tel: 0191 384 4263
www.tracyafranklin.com
Specialist goldwork threads, workshops, classes and courses

STITCHBUSINESS
Julia Triston and Tracy A Franklin
Studios 2 & 3
Fowlers Yard
Back Silver Street
Durham
DH1 3RA
Tel: 0191 383 0831 or 0191 384 4263
www.stitchbusiness.com
Independent Stitch School offering creative City & Guilds courses and masterclasses in design and art textiles in Durham City or by distance learning

Opposite page:
Green Circled (detail) (Rachel Gornall). Rachel's work is inspired by repeated shapes and patterns in nature. This piece was developed from observation of the endless repetition of circles in life under the sea. It is made from layers of hand-dyed cotton organdie, hand-cut patterns and stitch. Photograph: Colin Harvey. Below: **Armband** (Julia Triston). With cowrie shell tassels, from the Banjara tribe, India.

Index

Acknowledgements

Julia and Rachel would like to thank the following people: Joan Baker, for her editing suggestions and constructive comments on the first draft; STITCHBUSINESS students who have generously contributed their fabulous sketchbooks, design work and textiles; fellow members of Fusion for the loan of work and inspiration and fun in the last ten years of exhibiting together; all other contributors, including members of Prism, The 62 Group of Textile Artists and The Textile Study Group, who have given us permission to include their inspirational textile art work in this book. All photography by Steven Landles, except for: Julia Triston (pages 3 [bottom], 20 [top], 36, 37 [bottom], 38 [top left], 41 [top left and right], 43 [left], 44–45, 52, 60, 63, 71, 77 [top], 78, 82, 90, 108, 120, 125); Rachel Lombard (pages 13, 73); Cas Holmes (pages 22 [bottom left], 55 [bottom]); Colin Harvey (page 126); Lucy Barden (page 122); Mandy Pattullo (pages 22 [top left], 91); Michael Wicks (pages 50, 51).

Julia Triston is a professional artist, designer and lecturer in stitched textiles and contemporary art and design techniques. She has established a vibrant studio in the heart of Durham City where she teaches and creates her distinctive artwork. Julia has over 20 years' experience teaching in the creative industries, leading and delivering academic courses at all levels. Julia is co-director of StitchBusiness, an award-winning international stitch school specializing in City & Guilds courses and masterclasses in design, embroidery and stitched textiles. Julia is the creator of the Bra-ra dress and is known for the quirky use of raw materials, colour and embellishment in her textile work. Her work has been extensively documented and published in written and broadcast media. She exhibits and sells her work widely, and is an active member of the prestigious Prism textile group.

Rachel Lombard is an award-winning professional textile artist and designer who lives and works in County Durham. She has taught art, design and stitch techniques at FE colleges and community classes and is the internal verifier for all StitchBusiness City & Guilds courses. Rachel shares her passion for contemporary design and stitch through a programme of inspiring talks and workshops. Her artwork reflects her abiding interest in the creation and expression of individual, personal identity. Working predominantly with everyday and recycled papers, she uses colour, print and stitch to produce exciting, tactile surfaces and three-dimensional and functional items. *Stitch*, *Classic Stitches* and *Flair* magazines have all featured her work. Rachel exhibits and sells her artwork and is an active member of Fusion and Interface Arts.

Also available:

Drawn To Stitch
Gwen Hedley
9781906388805

The Found Object in Textile Art
Cas Holmes
9781906388461

Experimental Textiles
Kim Thittichai
9781906388478

To receive regular email updates on forthcoming Anova titles,
email update@anovabooks with your area of interest in the subject field.

Visit www.anovabooks.com for a full list of our available titles.